How To Be Ferociously Happy

And other essays

By

Dushka Zapata

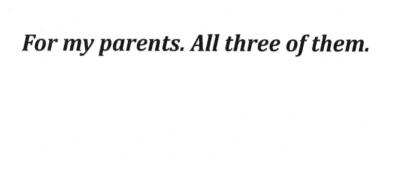

For my parents. All three of them.

There will come a time when you believe everything is finished.

That will be the beginning.

- Louis L'Amour

The Meaning of Life

I agonized over the Big Decisions until the day I realized big decisions were generally reversible and that it was the very small things that tended to have the most impact on the direction of my life. If I hadn't gone on that trip. If your photo hadn't caught my eye. If only I had picked up the phone on the first ring.

For a long time I believed that things happened for a reason until I witnessed my good friend's car flip over on the highway like a matchbox. He was so young and our story was just starting and I never got to see how it would end. I learned that things happen because they happen.

I believed that I had a purpose; that we all did. I have spent too much time watching people desperately trying to find this alleged purpose to the point that they are missing out on all the things that are right in front of them. A purpose that may or may not exist does not trump a life that you most certainly already have.

I was sure that I could manifest what I wanted. And sometimes it felt that way, but sometimes it didn't. Maybe I wasn't manifesting right.

My dad got sick. As absurd as this might sound to you I believed he was invincible. I was certain that the laws that applied to mortals did not apply to him. He got cancer and died a horrible death and I raged at the injustice and the cruelty of it all until I understood. People die.

Forget about greatness. Forget about success. Forget about wondering why you are here. Forget about what you were meant to do.

Instead, open your heart until you hear it crack. Expect miracles, but keep them non-specific so they can fill you with wonder. Or, be disappointed.

Wake up in the morning expecting nothing and stretch and revel in that stretch. Drink coffee. Eat good food and sigh at how good it tastes.

Kiss a lot and make love often and open the window and try really hard and lose and be really, really frustrated.

Sleep a lot or stay up late or waste your time or read. Participate. Or stay in bed.

Be sad. Be desperately, irreparably sad and hear the sound of your insides shattering over you making the same mistake. Forgive. Forgive again. Forgive yourself.

I am not saying life has no meaning. I am saying the only meaning of life is to live it.

An Expert At Getting Lost

I am 46 years old.

By this I mean that I have been 20 and 25 and 29 (and everything in between.)

I have at every age been "anxious" to "figure it out".

If someone asked me what all these years have given me, I would say *"Hello. My name is Dushka, and I am an expert at getting lost".*

Fortunately for me, stumbling around feeling lost is the only way to accumulate the experience required in getting found.

Here is the big fat secret adults keep from younger people.

Ready?

The age where you think you will have everything figured out never comes.

It doesn't exist.

Everyone is convinced that happiness lies on the other side of "figuring it out".

Instead, happiness is now.

Figuring it out is supposed to be fun. It's why we are here.

Feeling like you are the only person who hasn't is an illusion created mostly by yourself.

Figuring it out is another expression for the pursuit of happiness.

Happiness is not *"when I turn 30"* or *"when I find a boyfriend"* or *"once I get a job"* or anywhere in the future. It's within the actual pursuit.

Resolve to make it an adventure.

We are all trying to find ourselves.

Here is why: finding yourself is a moving target. The world changes constantly. We change constantly. Once you find yourself you have to begin again.

So it's best that you start accumulating relevant experience.

Hurray to feeling lost at every age.

Everything Exists At Once

I'm an introvert. I love being alone.

When Boyfriend is traveling I shuffle around my apartment straightening things out, eating oatmeal and apples for dinner and staying up late writing. Bliss.

I miss him when he's out. I miss his noise and chaos, his smoky cooking and the piles of indistinguishable items he leaves in nonsensical places.

Dushka, you are thinking. *You are contradicting yourself. Do you like being alone, or do you like being with him?*

Yes.

I need space and I need him. Not one after the other. Both at the same time.

We are more comfortable when we take in the world in the form of a dichotomy.

You need to decide, don't you? Career or love?

Your friend, the one you can count on but who never shows up on time. Flaky or reliable?

And that relationship. Is it making you happy or is it making you crazy?

Yes.

Dichotomies are bad for you.

Here is why:

By giving in to either/or, you force yourself to choose.

Choice implies sacrificing what you didn't choose.

Why would you do that when you don't have to?

What if life is meaningful and meaningless, complex and simple, unfair and beautiful?

What if I told you death, dark and devastating, is replete with light?

What if I tried to explain that I feel both empty and fulfilled, a mix of apathy and raging motivation that doesn't let me sleep; heartbroken beyond repair, alive?

What if I declared (and I do), that I am logical and pragmatic and believe in things I know aren't true?

Why wouldn't we resist fracturing the world into antonyms, resolve to instead have it all, rather than insisting we must decide, one or the other?

The second problem with dichotomies is that they are not real. Put simply, if we assume dichotomies where there aren't any, we force ourselves to see the world as it is not.

I know this might be uncomfortable, but everything exists at once.

And in exchange for accepting to live in this discomfort, we can have it all.

Why Reading Is Important

Imagine a room within four brick walls.

It's comfortable and you have what you need.

But it has no windows.

This room is an ordinary life. Acceptable, but limited.

Reading is like creating a window.

A window means a breeze. It means light, and the sun shining in, and a view.

The view can be anything, anything you want. A beach, the sky, a story, history; soldiers ready to raise the alarm, a boy in a cabin, a beautiful woman with a long yellow dress, a tiger, desperate and hungry, trapped on a life raft.

You can look out at whatever you wish; and you can learn. Pick what you want to learn about: the entirety of world knowledge is at your fingertips.

The more you read the more you open windows in the brick walls until you are left with no bricks. Just a vast expanse full of everything you have chosen.

Now remove your favorite story.

Pack up the soldiers and say goodbye to the woman and watch

the tiger and the life raft drift away.

Shut out the light.

Close off the breeze.

Replace every brick.

Return to your life, acceptable, circumscribed and finite.

This is a life without reading.

Now, you ask, am I saying reading is better than real life?

Is it better to live, or is it better to read?

And I ask you: why should you be without either?

My answer is — both. Pick both. Open all the windows.

Beautiful World

Unfailingly I am moved to tears when I learn about stories of heroism after something horrible occurs.

We don't live in a terrible world. We live in a beautiful world where awful things happen.

And every time awful things happen the good in humans reveals itself in new, surprising, breathtaking ways.

The Purpose Of Stars

In every civilization people have looked up at the sky and seen patterns and meaning, come up with shapes, constellations, legends and mythology.

About a year ago I read an article in the New York Times titled *"Stalking the Shadow Universe"* where I learned that most of the universe is invisible.

Dennis Overbye, the author, puts it like this:

"Atoms, the stuff of stars, you and me, make up only 5 percent of the universe by weight. A quarter of it is made of mysterious particles known as dark matter, and the remaining 70 percent a mysterious form of energy called dark energy."

Nobody knows what this "dark energy" is.

Turns out nobody knows very much of anything.

The next time you look up and wonder what the purpose of the stars is, know that this question connects you with the rest of the human race across centuries, and that your guess is as good as any.

And maybe that is the purpose of the stars.

To make us look up and fill us with wonder.

How To Catch A Liar

Your relationship with your significant other is a cornerstone of your life. It's the person you wake up with and come home to. The person in the trenches with you in the battle we wage every single day. As such, a healthy relationship with this person is vital to your happiness.

There is one element crucial to this relationship: trust.

If you are spending any time at all attempting to catch this person in a lie, you are altering your behavior to make room for this endeavor.

You are affected by increasing self-doubt and are second-guessing your own instincts.

Your days are tainted by suspicion.

Your life is contaminated.

You already know how sticky this is: it's a form of addiction. You will set more important things aside to succeed.

There is built-in defeat in looking so desperately for something you don't want to find.

The cost is a lasting impact on your ability to trust.

No one should have to live like that. It's exhausting, and nobody wins.

You have three choices:

Sit down with your significant other and ask if he is lying.

Determine that your suspicion originates in your own insecurities and is unrelated to the other person. Work on yourself to eradicate unfounded jealousy or you will carry it with you into every relationship.

Realize that you are with someone you cannot trust and end the relationship.

Be Incompetent

Speaking a new language is about getting comfortable with the undeniable fact that you're going to make a fool out of yourself and resolve to do it anyway.

When it comes to a language, studying will only get you so far. A language is a living thing, pliable, adaptable. Studying cannot replace the practice that real life provides.

The very good news is that this skill — the ability to declare *"I'm going to be really clumsy at this, and that's OK!"* — will serve you well across all aspects of your life.

Being bad at something is the only way to be successful at it.

It's Possible

It's possible to love someone you don't like very much, possible to resolve it's better to never see him again.

You can hold this love for him within you, stored in your solar plexus, either still beating or indolent. You can leave it there, unattended, turn your thoughts to other things.

It's possible to like someone, like them a lot, and expect you will one day love them and then one morning accept love will never come.

You can be attracted to someone you neither like nor love, and feel yourself come alive with this pull that makes everything feel new, like pavement, black after a downpour.

You can be attracted to a stranger or someone you know very well is forbidden, off limits.

You can be attracted to anybody.

You can hate and love at the same time. You can like and not like at the same time. You can love someone you have not been attracted to in years and one day, maybe because of a trick of the light or the approaching storm or your recurrent insomnia, you can feel the return of that attraction you could have sworn was gone for good.

It's also possible for it to never come back, regardless of the weather or your erratic sleep patterns.

There is love at first sight and the love you feel for someone you have never met and the inability to love someone you know you should. It would be so much easier, everything would be, if you could only love him, wouldn't it? But, you don't.

Conversely, there is the love that makes no sense for you to feel that you, despite your best efforts, cannot extinguish.

It's possible to find in the smell of the person you love the only thing that ever feels like coming home.

All these things are possible because we are human, because we are poetry, because we are contradiction and because our own experience sets the rules for what's possible, not what anyone else confirms. No one. Only you.

You decide what's possible.

Enthralled By You

Ambrose Bierce, one of my favorite writers, defined *"bore"* as *"a person who talks when you wish him to listen".*

He also defined an *"egotist"* as *"a person of poor taste more interested in himself than in me."*

What I love about his word definitions, compiled in a book called <u>The Devil's Dictionary</u>, is that they manage to be biting, funny and true.

To his point, to be less boring, you have to show interest in something other than yourself.

But "bore", much like beauty, is in the eye of the beholder.

I find small talk and parties painfully boring (which in turn would define me as a bore in the eyes of the many people who love parties and small talk.)

I don't drink, I don't do drugs and I rarely stay up late (and I say "rarely" because I define late as 10:30 p.m. and sometimes I turn the light off at 11:00.)

For a long time I fretted about how boring I was and tried to force myself to go to parties to *"get out there"* and *"have some fun"*. I assumed there was something wrong with me until the day finally arrived when the possibility of being the most boring person on Earth caused me less horror than the thought of dragging myself to another party.

Today, when someone finds me boring all it means is we're not a good match.

Someone out there will be fascinated by the people you find boring and, no matter how boring you worry you are, someone out there will be enthralled by you.

Less Reflection

I know life is a privilege. But it's also a responsibility that can feel overwhelming.

It's hard to know where to start.

What am I going to do with mine?

How will I find all the things that are out there waiting for me, such as my "soul mate" and my "purpose"?

How can I be happy?

Here's an idea.

I will place all of these heavy things on the shoulders of a young relationship. You know, with my soul mate.

Because loving him as much as I do is clearly my purpose.

He will make me happy.

So, yeah. That didn't work out so well.

There are no shortcuts.

The best thing you can do for any relationship is establish one with yourself. Get to know the person that you are.

Look in the mirror. That is your soul mate.

What is it that you want to do with your only life?

What will make you happy? (Hint: Never another. This burden will crush any relationship.)

Here is a good test (for myself): How do I feel when I am alone for a day or two?

If it feels good I'm on the right track.

If it doesn't I need to figure out what it is I'd rather not feel.

Next step: I need to unequivocally identify my stories and my insecurities. If I don't, everyone becomes a mirror and reflects them back at me.

I cannot battle a thousand refracted shadows.

My example: men cannot be trusted.

This story is well rooted in my vital organs. It's not that I am reluctant to trust. It's more that I don't want my heart broken. This means innocent, ordinary acts are interpreted as suspicious behavior. I need to clean this up. I can't eliminate it but I can label it so that when it comes up I can recognize it.

Hello, darkness. I see you.

So here is my relationship advice: have one with yourself. Know yourself. Love yourself. Save yourself.

If this sounds selfish or narcissistic note that it's just the opposite: narcissism is about staring adoringly at your own reflection. Needing more. More reflection.

Loving yourself is about reducing the chances any of your debris will be reflected back at you. Less reflection. Looking past yourself so you can see another more clearly.

Only then can you share the wonders you have found within you with someone else.

Quitting Is For Winners

"Never, ever ever quit."

I understand the value of persistence and perseverance and don't want to make less of that.

But let me assure you that there is a huge lesson in knowing when to cut your losses.

Part of what makes a winner is the wisdom to know when to quit.

It's a valuable skill to avoid letting your ego get the better of you, to refrain from sinking more time or money or heart into things that will just not work out: that relationship or business or job or marriage.

Then you can take your energy and resources and put them into something worth your perseverance.

That Kid

The toughest job in the world has got to be being a parent.

The first time this became clear to me I was around fourteen. A friend and I were talking about the completely dysfunctional, often clueless, downright weird things mothers and fathers do. In monotone and with her gaze fixed on the horizon, she confided what hers had inflicted upon her. *"My parents love each other so much that I always come in second".*

That's when it hit me — no matter what you do, you're going to screw up your kids. (My hope is that you find this oddly liberating.)

I was raised by parents who got divorced (many times over.) Here is what I would tell parents about the impact of their decisions on their kids — not because I'm an expert or a doctor but because I was that kid.

1. Don't make decisions based on what is good for your children. Make decisions based on what is good for you. (This doesn't mean "completely disregard what is important to them". It means "put yourself first, them immediately second.") I know this sounds unforgivably selfish. But kids learn by example. Teach them to be happy by being happy rather than exposing them to parents who are always torn, confused, angry or resentful. (Don't know if you should be a stay at home mom or go back to work? Should you stay in your marriage for your

kids? See above.)

2. Examine what is driving the choices you are making. Is it love or is it guilt? If the force is guilt, don't do it. Guilt is corrosive and nothing good ever comes of it.

3. Change is good. It feels terrible and scary and confusing and nobody really likes it, but it's quite possibly the only thing in life that you can be certain you'll get a lot of. So many (wonderful, loving) parents strive to raise their children in a Stable Environment. I ask you — how can a kid become a person resilient to change if all they have ever known is stability? I'm not saying, "please mess up their lives". I'm saying that if you mess up yours and feel you're dragging them along for the ride, they will be OK.

4. Be honest. Maybe don't be explicit, but do tell the truth. If your 8 year old walks in on the immediate aftermath of a screaming, raging fight and asks wide-eyed *"What's going on?"* and your reply is *"Oh, absolutely nothing, honey, everything is peachy!"* you're not protecting her. You're teaching her that she can't trust the most basic, most fundamental of all navigation tools: her own intuition.

Besides, kids know everything. Every. Thing. They might not fully understand it, or be able to articulate it, but they know. They know you have secrets, that you hide things from them, even that sometimes you'd love to get away from them.

They don't tell you that they know because they are trying to protect you too.

Pay Attention

A man gets on a bus I'm on.

He's really drunk. Wasted. Trashed. Plus, you can't trust him. He's bad news.

I know this not because he's stumbling and slurring but because he's yelling that he's drunk, wasted, trashed; that we shouldn't trust him, that he's bad news.

You should pay attention to what people choose to tell you about themselves, because it's usually true.

Introvert At A Party

Every introvert wishes she could be more extroverted.

At least this way we wouldn't be judged.

Right?

Let me begin by getting the bad news out of the way: you will always be judged.

It's what people do.

Some love you and want to change you because they think they know what's best for you. (Only you know what's best for you.)

Others are unhappy themselves and judge others as a result. The happier you are the less time you have to judge.

This is a good time to remind you how important it is that you focus on yourself instead of judging others.

Please never do anything "so that people stop judging you." It's not just that you can't ever stop it. It's that you will let it rule what you do. You can't be guided by what deeply irritates you. You have to be guided by what makes you more you.

You don't really want to become an extrovert (unless that's what you already are.) You want to operate at your best (which implies realizing that who you are is what makes you awesome.)

Before I go to a large party, here are some tips that work for me:

I make a list of people that I am (sort of) looking forward to seeing and send them a message a couple of days before the event. I then add I am eager to talk about xxx (to set an informal agenda and escape the misery that is small talk.) The party then becomes a sort of meeting point instead of a place where I try to catch someone I don't really want to talk to.

I pick a corner (chair, table, hall) with lots of foot traffic and sit there. People walk by, say hello and join me. This means I talk to a handful of people instead of "working a room", and they come to me which I find more manageable.

I take a break by going to the bathroom, leaning my head against a (clean) wall and taking a few deep breaths. Sigh.

I bring a camera and take awesome photos and send them to the party organizers (or in your case the bride and groom, or your cousins). You can turn your photos into a small album, complete with captions. Introverts notice things. I bet you make the best album ever = best, most thoughtful wedding gift.

I sometimes photograph people in super happy moments when they don't know they're being photographed. I then walk over with their perfectly frozen happy moment and offer to email them the photo.

I go home early.

How To Enrich Your Vocabulary

My native language is Spanish.

I'm going to share with you the single most trusty tool I use to expand my vocabulary in English:

I use Spanish. (And vice-versa).

By way of example, I was writing something a few days ago and had already used the word "full". I needed a synonym, and I needed it *pronto*. Another word popped in my head (but, alas, not in the language I needed it in.) *"Repleto"*.

Ah, "replete"!

So, so many of the words you already know in one language can be played with in another.

A sweeping view is more beautiful if you say *panorama,* you can (and should) always reduce the *drama,* you can follow that *aroma*, eat right and avoid *anemia*, look for someone of your *calibre*, hide in an *enclave*, require a *parasol* for exclusive use in your *oasis*, put yourself in a situation you consider *favorable*, or be *implacable*, even *culpable*; consider my suggestions both *improbable* and *irresistible* (because hopefully they are), be *sociable* or *miserable*, definitely *sexual, carnal, cordial,* always *cultural*; you can be an *animal*, go to that *funeral*, keep things *general* and *impersonal*, like me put language on a *pedestal*, be *personal, provisional, irritable* or *flexible*, veto any *credo,* approach things with *terror* or with *humor*.

All the words in italics are exactly the same in English and Spanish. But these are just a few insignificant examples. There are so many more that you already use that would impress any native English speaker.

Flex your beautiful, beautiful languages.

Something To Consider

My friend Sandy had been married less than two months when she found out her husband was dying of kidney failure.

A kidney transplant saved his life, and over the past four years I have been a witness to what this did for them.

They are grateful every day for this gift that granted them another chance at life and are incredibly active in their effort to pay it forward and improve the life of others.

After seeing the impact of organ donation I registered to be an organ donor. It's so hard to imagine what will happen to me after I die, but if I can I want to leave for others the gift of life.

A single person making this decision can save or dramatically improve the lives of 50 people.

Consider becoming an organ donor.

It will have a positive impact on many people and all those who love them.

How To Be Ferociously Happy

Happiness is elusive. You won't find it if you go looking for it.

Instead practice the following:

Fully enjoy this moment right now. You'll miss your whole life if you don't. (Also, anxiety is too much future.)

When making decisions, let love guide the way rather than fear.

While you are at it, defy fear. Look at it in the eye and do it anyway. (I trust you know the difference between brave and foolhardy.)

Accept things the way they are. This implies letting go of any expectations and resistance. (When you've mastered this, tell me how.)

Don't covet what you don't have. This means no envy (wanting for yourself what someone else has) or jealousy (the fear someone will take what is yours.)

When you come across an obstacle, feel challenged instead of frustrated. It's a matter of attitude/perspective.

Think of others. Happiness does not come from living inside your head or thinking only of yourself.

Relinquish trying to control everything. No forcing, pushing, pulling, manipulating, plotting. You can't control it all. (Believe me. I've tried). It's exhausting, and I hate to break it to you, but things tend to work out fine without your intervention.

Believe that what happens happens in your best interest. This is the true definition of surrender. Not giving up but trusting things will work out.

Because of my personality this tends to be my last resort but when I find myself here I am on my knees (literally — on my knees with my forehead on the floor) and feel truly peaceful.

Practice feeling overwhelming amounts of gratitude. I am not religious and feel like gratitude is the closest I have felt to God.

Decide that you have enough.

When met with the unknown, tap into a sense of adventure rather than uncertainty.

Resolve to see beauty everywhere.

Just Because You Are You

You can't "get" someone to like or love you. They do or they don't.

Conversely, you don't have to do anything to be loved. When you are liked or loved it happens just because you are you.

The Worst Mistake

Here is an excerpt of an article I read on November 5th, 2015 in the SFist:

A 30-year-old Seacliff resident was led away in handcuffs Wednesday after witnesses say she slammed her SUV into two boys who were crossing a Marina District street of San Francisco.

It was almost 8:30 Wednesday morning when the two 12-year-old 7th-graders at Marina Middle School were walking in the crosswalk on Bay Street at Buchanan.

According to San Francisco Police Department, an ice cream delivery truck had stopped in the westbound lane of Bay Street to allow the kids to cross, but the 30-year-old SF resident passed the truck on the left and struck the kids from behind the wheel of her white SUV.

The collision was hard enough that "the boys were launched into the air by the impact, thrown across the intersection. Their backpack, clothes, and shoes left scattered in the street."

She "was arrested at the scene" on suspicion of driving under the influence of alcohol or drugs" and was led away in handcuffs.

I have made many, many mistakes in my life. (I don't even know where to start, so I'll shoot for chronological).

I fought with my brother over toys, lied to my parents, trusted the wrong person, hated school, cut class, flunked every possible subject, and disappointed the very teacher who believed in me.

I projected all my fantasies (I'm prone to fantasies) onto a quiet boy only to realize he was not anywhere close to what I made him up to be (He did introduce me to Led Zeppelin and AC/DC so I guess this unfortunate incident had redeemable qualities).

I met a guy I knew all along was wrong for me and married him anyway. I met the right guy and married him and made every mistake in the book, despite of which we have remained friends, which goes to show you I at least chose well. And I could go on but it's time to make my point.

My point is: our mistakes are our mark, our adventure, our flavor. They are the only way we ever learn anything; the only tool we have to design our life.

Unless.

Unless what we do is irreversible.

Unless we do something that will forever derail us and others, like that 30 year old driver in the white SUV.

Do not ever think "you are OK" to get behind the wheel of a car if you have had anything to drink. You might do something you will regret forever.

There is no coming back from that.

That is the biggest mistake.

No Such Thing

How often do you go through something frustrating, sad, boring or time consuming and realize later that it was the key for something perfect later on?

This can only mean one thing: there is no such thing as a waste of time.

Why We Fight

I told Boyfriend I'd be home by 9:30 and it's 10:00 and I'm still at the restaurant with people from work.

I am normally extremely punctual and when I look at the time on my phone I cannot believe it.

I text him and he doesn't reply.

I hope he's not worried.

I hope he's not angry.

I hop in a cab and get home about an hour after I said I would. I feel frantic.

I come into the house. He's at his computer.

"I am sooo sorry" I say. *"Sooo sorry."*

He looks at me, perplexed.

"What happened, sweetie?"

"I don't know" I say. *"I guess I just lost track of time."*

He glances at the time. Turns back to me.

"Oh" he says *"It's fine! I hadn't noticed it was late!"*

"I texted you and you didn't reply."

"My phone's upstairs."

Boyfriend had no idea I was late.

I thought he'd be mad at me but I am the one who's mad at me. Losing track of time is out of character for me and I feel so careless.

I'm also feeling a bit dejected that Boyfriend barely noticed I was gone.

I expected he'd be worried. In my family worry equals love.

In my experience, we fight for two reasons:

Projection (where you project onto the other person something you are feeling towards yourself).

Expectations (when you are expecting something the other person has no idea about and therefore cannot meet it).

It's natural to assume these things are solved with communication but you can't really talk about something you don't know you are doing.

Awareness helps. The more we recognize our projections as such, the more we realize how we compare another person's actions with expectations we have never voiced or had not realized we had, the more peaceful relationships become.

A Gift To Yourself

It's so easy to believe life is a ferocious competition.

That we can only get what we want by being more aggressive.

That the notion of the zero-sum game is accurate: another person's gain is our loss.

Being kind can seem almost foolish.

None of these things are true.

Resolving to be kind is a gift to yourself.

Beyond the fact that it lifts your spirits, it changes the story you tell yourself, and as such it will change your life.

Being kind can (and most often does) change another person's day or outlook.

The more you give, the more you have.

The more you help another, the stronger your team and the stronger your network: another person's gain becomes your own. I don't mean only spiritually. I mean it factually.

Being kind is like a muscle, and you should exercise it every day.

Being kind is a superpower, and it is always available to you.

Accomplishment/Productivity

I don't associate "accomplishment" with "productivity."

"Accomplishment" has a certain grace. It has heft. It's related to fulfillment.

I feel it most when I'm learning, even if my learning is clumsy or slow. In other words, accomplishment is not even about competence. Learning is its own delicious reward.

"Productivity" is more about generating something. In my insides the term feels industrial, almost mechanical. I think it lacks soul. I can get a whole lot done without ever feeling any deep satisfaction. I'm just shoveling a pile of stuff out of the way.

The reason this distinction matters is because we relinquish a big part of our life when we confuse the two.

We are convinced that there is something wrong with not being productive. It makes us feel anxious and guilty; like we will fall behind.

We have forgotten the value of rest, of sitting in silence, of doing nothing, even of sleep. The ultimate escape has become, rather than leisure, ensuring we are as busy as possible to keep this angst at bay.

High levels of ever increasing productivity do not leave behind a sense of accomplishment.

No wonder we feel empty and exhausted.

I'd say more about how toxic this pattern is, how pervasive, about how we have the freedom to change it, as it's mostly self-imposed.

Or write about the correlation between feeling accomplished and knowing when to set things aside and rest.

But I can't right now. It's past my nap time.

A Moment At A Time

I used to be an avid planner.

I have learned planning is futile.

We can't predict what we want, as it assumes we're not going to change.

Everything changes.

Plus, the future has so many variables we cannot see that the most accurate way to live life is to go by what would be the best choice right now.

If you make the best choice for right now, the future takes care of itself.

I have lived the past 15 years making the best choices I can make for myself based on what I want for the present, rather than sacrificing the present for a future that might or might not come.

I don't know where I will be in 10 years. I don't even think about it.

I'm happy where I am today, so I'm fairly sure 10 years from now I'll feel the same way, one present moment at a time.

Go To Bed

Don't listen to whoever said *"never go to bed angry"*. Seriously, go to bed.

It will all look better in the morning.

The Delusion Of Comparing Yourself To Others

Comparing yourself to others is so painful, and so useless: it's an illusion. You can't possibly know what is truly going on in someone else's life.

You are looking out when you should be looking in.

In other words, you are spending time and energy on your own delusions. They might or might not be real.

Please don't fall into the trap of assuming that things would improve if only you got a job — a promotion — material success.

There is nothing outside of you that will make this better. This requires an internal adjustment.

You need to exercise turning all the focus on yourself, what you want to accomplish and how you want to live your life.

The clearer you are on the nature of your own path, the less you will worry about what others are doing and the more you will realize that you cannot possibly desire, covet or miss out on what doesn't truly interest you.

You will understand and respect that things unfold differently for every one of us.

The busier you are working on you, your life and your happiness, the less time you will have to dwell on another's success other than to celebrate it.

You Just Can't

You can cheat death and ensure the person that you love lives forever if you carry his love inside and resolve to honor his life with your actions.

You can change the past as your perspective evolves and you interpret things differently.

You can grow a jungle in a desert if you practice the vision of the best possible outcome (instead of the worst case scenario.)

You can make it rain if you accept yourself the way you are and build your life from that foundation.

You can alter the course of a storm if you work through wrath and understand its true source.

You can never change another person. Not to "fix", "help" or "save" them.

People have their own internal weather. And everybody knows you can't change the weather.

Remember

Back when I was first created I was given a box full of tools intended to protect me.

Fear, denial and the ability to remember people's behavior are a few of the useful things I have found inside that box.

Sometimes, when I'm hurt, I reach inside and pull out a tool that is not in proportion to what caused me pain.

The trick is to use the right sized tool in the correct amount.

Here is an example.

I am particularly sensitive to being stood up. It makes me feel forgotten, like I don't matter. It also has a way of throwing a wrench into a day typically booked with meetings.

If someone stands me up, my initial instinct is to no longer do business with that person.

But, wait. Have I ever stood someone up? I have. I mix up things in my calendar, experience emergencies, have an important meeting run over.

And, is it possible that the person who stood me up is otherwise wonderful to work with?

Absolutely.

The resolution to no longer work with that person, while tempting, is too big of a reaction.

What if a person otherwise wonderful to work with stands me up more than once?

Then I need to trust that this will happen again: they are disorganized to the point they will frequently not show up.

If this is the case, I remember. As a result, I try not to put myself in a position where they standing me up can affect me. Rather than driving to a far away location I will meet them at my office; where instead of being in an environment where I can't do anything else I can instead hold other meetings, make calls or get work done while I wait.

Remembering that they have stood me up can be effective.

Another example: What if a person I consider a close, dear friend says things to me that are painful, not with the intent to orient me but to hurt me?

If in the name of our friendship I pretend this did not take place and it happens again I intentionally put myself in harm's way.

This is where I need to recognize that this particular relationship is toxic.

I will wish this friend no ill will. I will hope my friend finds happiness. But I won't let her be a part of my life.

Friends are supposed to love me, not hurt me.

According to the dictionary, a grudge is *a feeling of ill will or resentment*. Is my memory of what another does hurting me? Then it needs to be adjusted. I am not supposed to be causing pain to myself.

But what if it's just the reminder that people can be trusted to be who they already showed you they are, and this keeps me safe?

If this is the case, it's best to remember.

Big Decisions

Before making any big decision surround yourself with
elements that defy reality (art, a book, a show).

There is such magic in the world that your perspective will be
more accurate if you blur the borders of what you currently
consider possible.

The Best They Can

I believe that most people are doing the best they can.

I have a hard time believing that anyone gets up in the morning thinking "today is a great day to be a mediocre girlfriend."

No one sets out with the intention of being (for example) a crappy parent.

Or decides that the way to go is to be a second rate friend.

I don't think anyone begins by feeling it would be OK to make an inferior effort.

It is no one's goal to be indistinguishable.

Life is tough. Patience runs out. We have difficult days, exasperated days. We take wrong turns. We make mistakes and bad decisions.

We very often — I very often — do a shoddy job.

On that day, a shoddy job was the best I could manage.

Here is what is most salient: My life improves dramatically when I begin by giving the other person this benefit of the doubt.

Instead of feeling insulted, hurt or wronged by whoever did not meet my (often unvoiced) expectations, I tell myself they were doing the best they can.

This changes my outlook: from feeling disappointed to feeling compassion.

More often than not, it turns out to be true.

Believing that people are doing the best they can is a better way to go through life.

Walking In Their Shoes

You don't really understand *anything* until you experience it.

I am an immigrant. I was born in one country, left, and now live in another. If you haven't left your country to go live somewhere else, you simply don't know what it's like.

I watched many, many movies — even documentaries! — where people get mugged. When someone put a gun to my head I realized I had no idea how having a gun to your head feels, not until it happened to me. The world stops. You are violently living in the present. At other times you might "practice mindfulness", but you have not experienced everything *ceasing to exist* until you feel cold metal pushing against your temple and see terror in the eyes of the person holding the gun.

My beautiful superhero of a dad was sick for two years. For those two years I witnessed his health deteriorate and felt as he was dying that I could anticipate what it would be like to lose a parent. Until he died, until I saw his still warm body wrapped and taken away, I had no idea.

I speak multiple languages. I cringe when I see a poem translated from a language that I speak to another that I also speak. Translations — even by world renowned translators — inevitably fall short. I am very happy people have a chance to experience poetry in other languages, but it's just a shadow of the original. If you don't speak Spanish, you don't understand

Borges.

I once read that one of worst things that happen to homeless people is that they feel invisible because no one ever looks into their eyes. I have never been homeless. It would change the way I perceive the world.

I'm not black. I cannot fathom the experience of being racially profiled. It angers me to imagine it, and that is not the same.

I have never had a one night stand. I have never had twins. I have never been to war. I have never been a mother. I have never walked on the moon. I have never had cancer. I have never kissed a woman. I have never engaged in group sex. I have never been obese. I have never done drugs. I have never battled addiction or experienced withdrawal.

I have never felt unloved.

The only way to change the world is to understand it, and only through someone who has actually experienced something can we ever come close to walking in their shoes.

Go For It

Many wonderful things that have happened to me I once considered "a long shot".

If you regard something as a long shot, go for it anyway.

Irreparable

Divorce is not like a break up. It's way more complicated. It's like a black hole in the center of your existence that sucks everything in: your family, your friends, your life.

When you get married you build. You embark on it with a sense of it being a huge, life-affecting decision that impacts everything. You exist within concepts like "forever".

If marriage is the creator, divorce is the destroyer.

Divorce is just as big as marriage, but a reverse flow. It's intended to undo the love you've built, tear down, eliminate, pack in.

It's the opposite of the creation of a beautiful life.

Divorce is devastating. This devastation is less related to the loss of another (although it very much is) and more related to what you confront in relation to yourself and your own (previously largely invisible, murky) flaws and shortcomings.

I had an extremely amicable (even loving) divorce. We never, not once, argued over anything legal, practical or financial. We were never underhanded or hurtful. My ex-husband is now one of my closest friends.

Still, I mourned.

Still I feel like something inside me will never be the same.

Noise

Figuring out what is the best way to be living your life is like trying to listen to soft music in a room with deafening noise.

You need to stop listening to all the noise and start listening to your own soft music.

The noise comes from people who feel they know what is best for you. Mostly they are very well intentioned, but here is the thing. They are not you. They are your parents, your family members, your friends, your boss, even your own brain (once it internalizes all the noise).

Noise sounds like this:

Why is everyone doing better than me?

Will that choice make you money?

Should you really be doing that?

Sure, it looks fun but you could get hurt.

Be careful.

You are not doing it right!

You are not good enough.

What will other people say?

Do you really think you can make a career out of that?

But that's not what's best — what my parents would want — the reasonable option!

The way to listen to your soft music is to pay attention to how things make you feel:

That thing you like makes you elated or excited or giddy or you feel dread.

Or pay attention when the soft music uses your body to try to tell you what not to do:

The appointment you are always late for.

The document you just can't write.

The recurring headache.

Insomnia.

Restlessness.

Anxiety.

In my opinion, listening to that soft music and not listening to everything else will show you the way.

The more you fine-tune your listening, the easier it becomes.

No Small Thing

Anytime you wonder if you can lie about small things to make yourself look better, reconsider.

The small things are always the big things, because they show you are willing to lie about things that are not that important.

It undermines trust.

People have a lot of problems trusting someone who choses to lie, in particular about inconsequential things.

It's In There

Have you ever seen the seed of a redwood tree?

Sequoia Sempervirens. It's nothing short of a miracle. A minuscule, hard, unassuming package that contains — not the potential (such a tired word, bland promise, assumption that weighs the recipient down with a vague sense of having to do something grand, but what?) but the *ingredients* (affirmative, inarguable, scientific, like chemistry) — needed to become one of the most majestic forms of life on the planet.

Have you ever visited a redwood tree grove? It's a thousand times more powerful than the most impressive man-made cathedral (with my respectful apologies to St. Peter's Basilica).

Redwoods are the largest organism the world has ever sustained. They are so big that when you stand up against one, hug it (do it) and look up, it blocks out the sky.

The seed of a redwood tree does not sprout easily. It needs a combination of very specific conditions. All of what you would expect: nutrient-rich soil, and water, and humidity.

But here is the astonishing thing: a redwood seed cannot germinate without fire.

A redwood tree is so much more than what you see, even if what you see is nearly overwhelming in its splendor and dignity. It's actually a vertical universe (Richard Preston, in his magical book The Wild Trees, calls it *a vertical Eden*). These trees, older than most human monuments, have a kingdom of plants and animals living in their branches, lichens and ferns and salamanders that cannot be found in any other ecosystem. In Preston's words *"Their mysterious canopies are rich with hanging gardens, blackened chambers hollowed by fire, and vast, aerial trunk systems fused into bridges and towers".*

The purpose implicit in the seed of the redwood is not just a redwood tree, but a glistening green planet teaming with life in its endless combinations.

What is my point here? My point is that we each have a similar kernel of divinity, indestructible and perfect, within each of us. That its magic branches out into everything we set out to build: our lives, our relationships and families and careers.

This force inside all of us could be dormant, waiting for the right conditions to unfurl into something so extraordinary that it would be impossible to grasp or even begin to understand.

But it's there. In you. In me. You just wait and see.

Self-Confidence

There is no faster way to develop self confidence than facing your fears.

I don't mean putting yourself in the way of harm (like walking in a dangerous neighborhood at night) but rather life related fears.

Big ones (such as falling in love) and little ones (such as ordering something for lunch you've never tasted).

Every time you do something you didn't think you could you something shifts inside you.

Suddenly you know what it feels like to be proud of yourself.

Worth Loving

I miss my ex-husband. I miss his simple and elegant view of the world, his gentle disposition, our easy relationship and who I was when I was with him.

I love my boyfriend, his noise and social grace, how when we're together we are almost always laughing, frequently at ourselves.

These two places in my heart neither touch nor threaten each other.

I have no interest in going back to being romantically involved with my ex (and neither does he) and the fact that I miss him and always will does not affect how full and true my love is for Boyfriend.

I have spent too much time trying to read the signs of exactly how high the risk is of losing someone I love.

No one should have to live like that.

In an effort to put myself out of my misery I looked everywhere for the real measure of that risk.

I peered into every photo of his ex, studied the glint in her beautiful eyes and her shiny, straight blond hair.

There they are, squinting in the sun.

I scrutinized the inflection of his voice when he spoke about the women who came before me.

He mumbled in his sleep and I listened intently for hints or the mention of someone else's name so that in the full light of day I would not be surprised.

Please don't break my heart.

I finally figured out that my fear and my doubts did not reside in the man I was with nor in any of the women who came before me.

The person I was doubting was myself.

We all need to work on loving ourselves instead of trying to decipher anyone's feelings about anybody else, which is like emptying out the ocean with a teaspoon.

If you look hard enough for evidence you will find it even if it doesn't exist.

It's so much easier to completely trust that I am worth loving.

Because You Make It So

Something happens to you. Maybe something terrible.

You break it off into smaller pieces so you can analyze it.

You ask yourself as many questions as you can:

What good did this bring?
What did I learn from this?
How did it develop my compassion or empathy?
How did this play a role in me becoming stronger?
How can I turn this into an advantage?

It is my belief that it's healthy and in your best interest to reverse engineer what happens to you so that you come to understand. So that you can put some order into that terrible thing.

This exercise is empowering. It removes you from the temptation of perceiving yourself as a victim.

Everything that happens happens for the best because you make it so.

Because making it so will contribute to your growth and your happiness.

Because it's the only way to make sense of awful things.

Escondidillas

When I was little we used to play this game in Mexico called *Escondidillas.*

Picture a group of kids in a room.

One of them is blindfolded and turns to the wall and counts to ten.

The others quickly hide an object somewhere in the room.

The blindfolded kid has to find it. He walks around. As he gets closer to the hidden object others yell *"Warmer! You are getting warmer!"* If he walks further from the object everyone yells *"Colder! Colder!"*

It stands to reason then that if you were the one blindfolded and started walking in one direction and everyone yelled *"Colder!"* you'd immediately turn and start walking in the opposite direction.

The voices only yell *"warm"* or *"cold".* Not *"Hey! You're getting warmer but this is not what your parents would want!"* Not *"You're getting warmer but you will make tons more money over in the other direction!"* Not *"Colder but keep going because it will make you more desirable to the opposite gender!"* Not *"Oh my God! Warmer, but what will people think!?"*

Now, as an adult, don't listen to anything anyone else tells you. Walk away from colder. Walk towards warmer.

Put It Down

All my life if I started a book and didn't like it, I would finish it anyway in the name of discipline.

Now I feel like the power of discipline needs to be put to better use.

If something doesn't elate you, don't stick with it. Life is short.

Everything I Need To Learn I Learn In Yoga

Here are a few of the things it taught me:

Who you are shows up everywhere.

Often, I come to a pose I can't do.

And think *"I will never stand on my head. It defies gravity."*

About six months later, there I was in my mid-forties, holding a tripod headstand in the center of the room. I realized that anything that seems impossible — anything — would become easy, because that is what happens when you practice.

Practice, and all will come.

Once your brain has grasped that, it extrapolates it to other areas of your life (without you telling it to).

"I don't think I can ever do that" becomes you surprising yourself with all you can do.

Let go of what doesn't serve you.

What you're thinking is *"Of course! But, how?"* And the answer is: I don't know. But if you focus on your breath instead of your thoughts, and you want to stop holding on to something that hurts you, one day it will loosen its grip on you.

Breathing in and out through your nose doesn't just calm you. It changes you.

You want a better explanation. But that would be intellectual, and you are not your thoughts. You are their creator, and sometimes, for a glorious, lucid instant, their observer.

Yoga works not with you the thinker, but with you the witness.

With your thoughts out of the way, things have space to get sorted out.

You don't need to know how.

You are not making it happen. It happens on its own.

Stop thinking.

Thoughts are meant to be your servant. If you let them be the master, they will lead you astray. They will betray you. They will make you suffer.

If you, like Descartes, are convinced that is why you exist, this practice reminds you that everything you could need — even the cure to loneliness — is already inside you.

It's just that it doesn't reside where you think.

How can this be easier?

There you are, locked in a bind. And the teacher asks — "how can it be easier?"

What if I told you to relax when you felt you needed to struggle? You don't have the stamina to muscle your way into everything. That's when the energy you're expending that you don't need to be expending reveals itself. Why is your jaw clenched? Why are you putting all the weight on the tips of your toes?

Look at yourself. Look at your job. Look at your relationships.

How can it be easier?

How can you work harder?

And of course, the reward. How can you work harder? Certainly not clenching your jaw. But once your jaw is relaxed you have more energy to put into where it matters.

In lifting from the upper back.

Or, anywhere.

How can you be comfortable within uncomfortable situations?

Have you ever held plank for more than a couple of minutes?

When the teacher says you can "drop to your knees" you want to flop on your stomach.

You learn that while it hurts, that's ok. While it's hard, that's ok.

Soon you stop desperately trying to escape other uncomfortable situations.

Less flailing (which is in itself exhausting).

More acceptance.

Whatever you push pushes you back.

I used to believe pushing was the only way to get things to work out the way I wanted them to (OK. I still do. I have to re-learn anything I think I've already understood).

And there I was, trying to touch my toes, frustrated with myself for not "doing it right".

"Don't push", said my teacher. *"Whatever you push will push you back."*

(Whoa.)

Surrender.

This concept is counter-intuitive to anyone who believes you have to fight for what you want (Like me).

Surrendering and trusting — having faith — that whatever is happening is happening in your best interest, and that things will unfold as they should without the need for you to interfere.

Surrender is always my last resort (because it's not in my nature) and I feel awash with gratitude when, despite my tendency to refuse its solace, I always find it there waiting for me.

Meeting people where they are at.

And on a related note, don't try to change the other person's mind, opinion, or outlook. In fact, don't try to change the other person. Stop trying. It doesn't work. It never will. It never has.

(There. That should free up more energy to put into other things.)

Multitasking. As in, don't do it.

I often go into a class dragging work (or whatever it is I'm dragging) in with me. The teacher says, "Whatever you have to do won't get done while you are here. Focus on breathing and moving through the poses".

It hits me that I can take time off from whatever weighs on me any time I want.

Let me say it in another way, because it's amazing: if you do one thing at a time, you can take a break from everything else.

Getting off the roller coaster.

There isn't room for your ego on the mat (you'll get injured fast by doing something everyone is doing if you aren't ready for it).

In yoga, you are strong one day and you suck the next.

You eventually learn to feel equal regard towards the powerful you and the sucky you.

(You might not believe me, but I assure you both of you are already perfect.)

And my favorite thing for last.

Being better requires minuscule steps.

One of my teachers asks: *Can you go a bit lower? Can your back be a little straighter? Can you breathe just a bit deeper?*

Stretch.

It's such an incredible concept. Think about it: Depression makes you want to curl up. Darkness makes you shrink. Fear makes you wither. Stubbornness makes you narrow. Hate makes you lessen. Guilt makes you contract. Regret makes you shrivel. Negative feelings constrict. They diminish you. Stretching opens up your heart. It fills you with strength. It makes you more flexible. And it doesn't take much. You don't need time to learn how to get everything just right.

There already is beauty and power inherent in you.

Because it is inherent in everything.

Why Make The Bed?

Whenever you wonder if your logic is sound, try seeing what happens if you multiply it/extrapolate it/apply it to everything.

Why make my bed if I will crumple it come evening?

Why make friends if we will fight?

Why be born if I will die?

Why trust if someone will betray me?

Why eat delicious morsels of juicy perfection if I will get hungry again?

Why be happy if I will end up sad?

A lot of painful things will happen if you live.

Live anyway.

Gossip

When I was six my friend told me she wasn't allowed to come over to my house to play because my parents were divorced.

She said the word *"divorce"* like it was dirty.

I went home and asked my mom if divorce was contagious.

Despite what everyone was saying, my parents went ahead and split up anyway.

This is how I learned very early in life that the pursuit of your own happiness trumps what anyone may or may not be saying about you.

This incident occurred about 40 years ago. In that time, I've learned a lot more about gossip.

Here is a summary:

People talk less about you than you think. They have the audacity to be too preoccupied with themselves to be concerned about you.

Why do people gossip? Because tearing someone else down is evidence that you are unhappy with a part of your own life. The happier you are, the less you will criticize someone else, and the more empathy you will feel for what they are going through.

What someone says about you when they are unhappy with

themselves is more about them than it is about you. As such, it's not ever a good guide for how to live your life. Don't make decisions based on what others might think or say. It will steer you wrong every time.

The busier you are working on you, your life and your happiness, the less time you will have to talk about others.

And even better, the less time you will have to show any concern for what others say about you.

I am a deeply flawed person. I have a lot of work to do and as such I have no time to waste.

Yes They Do

Saying *"people don't change"* is a cop out. It's so defeatist. It's more than just pessimistic. It's fatalistic. It's like saying there is no point to the exercise that is life.

It's turning your back on you, on your ability to be better, to grow, to learn the lesson. It's giving up on the (flawed, but oh, so hopeful) human race.

I've heard *"people don't change"* so many times that it never occurred to me to question it. But, guess what? I know for certain that people do. I'm the closest person I can point to.

Moving to another country changed me. My work changed me. I know that in many fundamental ways I'm the same person I used to be twenty years ago, but also know that in other — equally fundamental ways — I'm not the person I used to be. Sometimes for the worse, but mostly for the better.

People change through being dedicated to something. They change when they are loved. They change when they decide it's time to, when whoever they are is just not working anymore.

Of course, change is not always a good thing. People often change for the worse.

All I'm saying is that if it's possible for people to change for the worse, then it's at least just as likely for people to change for the better.

The Fracture Within

A lot of people think that loneliness is something that happens outside of you: the assumption is you are lonely when you don't have company.

But one can feel lonely in a room full of people, even loving people. One can feel lonely in a relationship.

Conversely, a person can live alone and never feel lonely.

It took me years to understand that loneliness is a fracture within, not an external characteristic of our lives.

We assume we will feel less lonely as soon as we find our ever elusive "soul mate"/a good friend/as soon as our significant other finally understands us.

The epidemic of loneliness we all blame on social media really comes from being convinced it's an outside ailment we believe we can fix or treat and are therefore attending to it in the wrong places (Out there, and some day). I think bouts of loneliness are inherent to the human condition. It's again the assumption that we need something we'd get if only.

Everything we need we already have. It was inside us all along.

Don't Worry

Worry is a colossal waste of time.

It prepares you for nothing (even if you worry full time you can't possibly predict every bend and curve life tends to come with).

It ensures you suffer the most: all the times you assume something is going to happen, plus when it does (If it ever does).

It's bad for your health, increases your stress levels, exhausts you. It causes you to lose sleep and clouds your judgement.

Plus I believe that most of what you worry about never actually takes place.

There are better things to do with your most valuable resources: your energy, your intelligence, your imagination. Use those resources instead to visualize the most incredibly wonderful outcomes.

Worry is not a character trait. It's a habit. It can be broken.

Grace

More than "keeping it all under control", more than "being right", even more than finding the perfect word, what I want is to learn how to handle things with grace.

It has the best aftertaste.

How To Be A Good Girlfriend

Truth1:

I have been known to fight with Boyfriend *in my head.* He does something irritating and I practice our conversation — both my points and his imagined responses — to rehearse different possible scenarios.

By the time he comes home I'm all worked up.

Over an argument that never actually took place.

Truth2:

Once I got angry at Boyfriend because of a relationship *that happened before he met me.* Because, I'm sometimes jealous of his past.

I am afflicted by retroactive jealousy.

I could go on, but instead I'll get to the point.

To be the best girlfriend I can be, I need to figure out what all my stories are, and exactly what my insecurities are.

Because most of the times that I am mad at Boyfriend my anger is not related to him but to my own history.

I concluded a long, long time ago that all men would eventually cheat. Not because men can't be trusted, but because I didn't want to get hurt.

Another person cannot fight the gigantic, invisible defense mechanisms you've set up (deliberately or not) around your heart.

To me, ordinary, every day acts can appear to be "evidence".

To him, my behavior can be utterly irrational.

It's my job — my own process — to make a distinction between my stories and what is actually taking place so I don't fight about things that haven't occurred.

And so I don't drag these fights with me into every single relationship.

If Boyfriend comes home late one day I look at my insecurities straight in the eye.

I see you. You are a delusion. Thank you for trying to protect me. You can go now.

That's what you can do to be a good girlfriend. Know yourself. So you can see others for who they are rather than warped through the lens of your own insecurities.

Your Inner Guide

In my experience, what you think you want comes to you in words.

I want to buy a house.

I want to get married.

I want to have children.

I want to make a good salary.

I want a promotion.

Your inner self uses your body or your feelings to express itself.

You are suddenly excited.

Your hands are sweaty.

You feel a hole in the pit of your stomach.

You feel queasy.

You can't sleep.

You lose your appetite.

You want to run.

Or, you experience an internal rebellion.

You are good in school and there is this important test you keep flunking.

You have an important interview and you have never been late in your life and you can't seem to make this one on time.

You have a headache — for real — every time the guy you are supposed to love asks you out on a date.

In my opinion, you should listen to your feelings.

Even when you can't explain them.

You should pay attention to what your body is trying to tell you.

Many people say that what you think you want makes sense; and your inner self is capricious and crazy and you shouldn't listen.

It's just the opposite.

Your inner self does not know about logic and doesn't live in a world ruled by social constructs; so to your thoughts it sounds like your inner self makes no sense.

When really, it's your thinking that needs to put into words the messages your feelings and your body are sending, like this:

"I can't explain how I know this because it seems like a great opportunity, but I'm not going to that interview because I will end up in the wrong job."

"Don't ask me to make sense of this, but that guy described as 'a really good catch' is not someone I am interested in."

"I don't care why; but I really want to take that dance class so I'm going to. The thought of dancing makes me happy."

Your guide is what you call your inner self.

Your thoughts are supposed to translate and figure out how to get you there.

Go Find Them

Have you ever noticed how beautiful someone (friend or lover) looks as you come to love them?

From this I infer that beauty has little to do with physical attributes.

And that if someone doesn't think you are beautiful you should go find all the people who do.

How To Know If You're An Adult

Maturity is knowing —

That being special does not entitle you to special treatment.

That "adult" doesn't exist and the age to *really* be one keeps moving out as you get older.

That it's possible to make all the right decisions and end up with an undesired outcome. Ergo, the outcome should not be the measure of if you made the right decisions.

That everyone's number one concern is themselves, not you.

That nothing is personal. It's not all about you.

That there is no such thing as blame. It's all you.

That as you give to the world the world gives to you.

That the world owes you nothing.

That winning an argument with the people who are important to you is really shortsighted.

That being there for the people that you love is what it's about and it's mostly for you.

That life is more about creating things and less about finding things. Less about fairy tales and more about working at it. This applies to the prince and the knight and the horse and the sparkling ring and the princess dress and your soul mate and to happily ever after.

That there are no shortcuts.

That closing yourself off is the worst thing you can do because it will kill you before you die. Give. Give give give. If you are used, give. Love. Love love love. If you are hurt, love.

That you feeling that you are behind compared to others, that another person has more than you, is luckier than you, has a better life than you, is nothing but a story you tell yourself.

That you have less time than you think.

That you will not get away with anything: you will pay for every bit of harm you inflict on others and on yourself. Not in some afterlife. Right here. I don't mean cosmically. I don't mean karmically. What I mean is that you reap what you sow. Everything you do has consequences.

That silence is indispensable.

That it's a beautiful, beautiful world and it's up to you to see.

Choose Love

You cannot protect yourself from all the things that could hurt you. I can pretty much guarantee that you will be hurt again and again.

But, you have had horrible break-ups and you survived. Which is a good indicator that you can trust yourself to make it through another one.

So, thank your fear for trying his best to take care of you. Tell him you appreciate that he exists, but that he is only one of your many advisers, not your master.

Show your fear, every time he shows up, who is boss.

Tell your fear that he is welcome to tag along, but to keep his voice down to the faintest of whispers.

Listen to that (by now) nearly inaudible whisper saying *"Don't love again! We will get hurt!"* and shout back *"I LIKE HER A LOT! I WANT TO LIKE HER SOME MORE!"* and then let your heart set the pace for how quickly you move into loving her.

If the choice is fear or love, chose love.

Make this choice again and again and again.

Self-Fulfilling Prophecy

I suffer from insomnia.

I know sleep is one of the pillars of good health and go out of my way to make sure I get enough.

If I have to get up very early the next day, I often lie in bed anxious that I won't be able to fall asleep.

The chance I might not be able to sleep keeps me up half the night.

This is a simple example of a self-fulfilling prophecy.

We obsess over what we fear to the point that we make it come true.

The thing to remember is this: If this is so (and it is) it stands to reason that the reverse is also true.

If you can create what you fear, you can create what you want.

Crucial Distinction

Most of Boyfriend's friends are women. I can understand why: If he wasn't my boyfriend I would definitely want him to be my friend.

In the very beginning of our relationship some of his friendships made me uncomfortable.

It didn't take long for me to understand that my discomfort and his behavior were not related.

His friends are just that and my tendency towards jealousy and suspicion precedes our relationship.

The best way to express trust and respect in any relationship — including the one with ourselves — is to learn to distinguish between our own emotional baggage and another's behavior.

The Expert Is You

Doctors know — and are reminded every day — that even at their most competent they are fallible.

The rest of us make the mistake of confusing doctors with deities, believing everything they say and putting all our medical decisions entirely in their hands.

The best thing you can do for yourself and for your medical care is to assume responsibility and be a team with your doctor.

The doctor is the medical expert and you (and only you) are the expert on yourself.

On this note, never confuse a medical diagnosis with your fate.

Doctors are frequently wrong. Just like the rest of us.

Mad At Me

Last night Boyfriend and I had a dinner party to go to. I didn't want to go (I'm an introvert and tend to prefer staying home).

Boyfriend told me he was going without me.

"You're mad at me!" I said. *"They are our friends and you think I should go. But, I've had a hard week at work and it's Friday and just want to stay home and read! There is nothing wrong with that!"*

"Đushka" he said. *"I'm not mad at all. You had a busy week and just got back from a grueling business trip. I completely understand you wanting to stay home".*

I realized that I was accusing my boyfriend of a feeling I was harboring for myself. I wanted to stay home but felt bad about missing my friend's dinner.

I was mad at me.

Welcome to one of the strangest, most pervasive phenomenons of our psyche.

You are what you don't like in others. What you see in others is you, projected onto another person. Hence why it's called "projection".

It's incredibly helpful to know that this exists.

Be careful when you get angry at someone. It might just be your projection and not at all what the other person intended or meant.

Listen closely to people when they talk about others. They are telling you about themselves.

You Don't Have To Fix It

When someone I love shares a problem with me, I have a nearly irrepressible urge to "fix it".

"I am worried I'm going to lose my job" a friend told me just a few weeks ago. *"And so many of my friends work with me so I'm also genuinely concerned losing my job will have an impact on my relationships".*

"You won't lose your job!" I said. *"You are so very good at what you do. But to make yourself feel more in control, why don't you start working on your curriculum? And, you are an excellent friend. Where you work won't matter to the people who love you."*

I was not listening.

Good listeners have absolutely no agenda.

They are propelled by nothing.

They have no intentions.

They are not:

Hearing but really thinking about what they are going to say next.

Figuring out how to coax, convince or present their case.

Attempting to "help" or "make the other person feel better".

Trying to find a solution.

Mixing in their own feelings or providing opinions.

Judging.

Reassuring.

Good listeners are just open.

Ears open, heart open, mind open.

Open to listening.

This is how good listeners grant you the greatest gift of all: the gift of feeling understood.

Remind me.

Secret Hurdles

There are a hundred things that are really hard for me that seem easy for others.

I overcome secret hurdles every day, which means others do too.

We live in a planet inhabited by people constantly executing furtive acts of the most intimate heroism.

You Can Do Anything

When you were born you took deep breaths right away. You proceeded to accomplish truly complicated things: you learned to walk and to talk and to write.

Have you ever stopped to consider how complex it is to learn a language? Each word has a meaning and you have to string them together and distinguish one from another in a stream of speech. You grasp subtle nuances too: like the difference between a glass and a cup — both contain a liquid, but they are not the same.

Language is daunting, and you did it.

I'm pointing out the fact that you already come equipped to be good at many things. It's just that some are automatic (like breathing), some we take for granted (like language), and some make you self-conscious (like kissing). In all of these cases, the ability to pick them up is a part of your original composition.

Trust that.

If you need further evidence, look back at the other incredible things you have already accomplished without much consideration.

Fallacy

"You can't change the past" is a fallacy.

As times goes by, our feelings and perspective change. We acquire new information, we learn how it is never anyone else's fault but our own.

All of this casts our already compromised, imperfect memories in a different light.

Nothing changes more than the past.

This means that you can transform the past from "bad experience" to something you needed to go through to be better and do better.

Practice

I practice yoga.

I very often come to a pose I can't do.

Say, a tripod headstand.

I sit there and think: *"Never. I will never stand on my head with my hands positioned like that. It defies gravity."*

But I keep trying. I attend more classes and observe the steps and try again and "fail" and then, a few months later, there I am, in my (late) forties, holding a tripod headstand in the center of the room.

I realize that anything that seems impossible — anything — becomes easy, because that is what happens when you practice.

Practice, and all will come.

Once your brain has grasped that in one part of your life (say, yoga) it extrapolates it to other areas of your life (without you telling it to).

"I don't think I can ever do that" becomes you surprising yourself with all you can do.

So whatever it is that you would like to be good at, practice.

Every Head Is A Different World

In Mexico we have a saying: *"Cada cabeza es un mundo"* (every head is a different world).

Have you ever read Oliver Sacks? He was a professor of neurology and wrote many incredibly beautiful books (and articles) about the experiences he came across, usually in the form of case histories.

One of his books, called <u>Awakenings</u>, was made into a movie with Robert De Niro.

Oliver Sacks died recently and wrote several insightful and poignant articles about his experience as he approached death.

Of all the books he wrote, my favorite is called <u>An Anthropologist on Mars</u> (I discovered it because I was visiting a friend's house and the lights went out. The book had a glow in the dark cover so I walked right to it and pulled it off the shelf).

In it he describes seven patients with extreme neurological conditions that have integrated their illness into their lives. They have all managed to be fully functional because of what they live with and not in spite of it.

The book is called <u>An Anthropologist on Mars</u> because he claims the worlds of each of his patients are so different from ours that it is akin to them living on other planets; planets he visits in order to better understand and learn from these highly adaptive personalities.

I believe we each live in a different world. It's only through getting out of your own head and putting others before yourself that you can, if only temporarily, pay a visit to another person's planet.

If you're lucky, you like the view and get to stay a while.

It Will Always Be Winter

Depression disguises its voice as your own.

It tells you it will always be winter. It tells you there is no good reason to live. It tells you nothing will ever again give you pleasure, not grass or cold water or an apple lovingly sliced into perfect wedges. It tells you it's not worth getting out of bed.

You can't do it, it says. *You are worth nothing and you are a burden to everyone and crawling out of this deep darkness can't be done so don't even try.*

Don't even try.

Depression deceives you into mistaking these thoughts for your own until you forget it's the depression talking and not you.

You think it's you, so you believe it all.

Less Overwhelming

The secret to achieving huge goals is to break the goal down into small steps, so small that the task becomes easy.

Small steps are less overwhelming, and they have a way of adding up in ways you wouldn't believe.

If I tell myself I want to write a book and am paralyzed by the task before me the book won't get very far.

If I tell myself I will write a page a day — or even a paragraph a day — the book will get done sooner or later.

Don't underestimate the power of small steps, and don't underestimate yourself.

How To Witness Magic

Have you ever heard of the zero-sum game?

The worst way to go through life is to assume that another person's gain is your loss.

This breeds jealousy and envy inside you; and kills collaboration, teamwork and happiness.

Assume instead that there is no joy like witnessing another succeed.

Go through life pulling others up every chance you get.

Watch magic unfold.

Who You Are

Emotions are beautiful but they don't define you.

The same goes for your thoughts.

You are not your thoughts. You are the person who witnesses them.

You don't need to break down your thoughts but rather separate yourself from them so you can see they are not who you are.

Sit in a quiet room and breathe in and out, in and out, as deeply as you can. Take your time. Take 10 slow, deep breaths. As you do, listen to your breath. As your brain returns to your thoughts (it always will), gently bring it back to your breath.

Do this for a few minutes every day.

Before you know it your thoughts will slowly but surely loosen their hold on you.

Shortsighted

This is what happens when I'm intent on winning an argument:

I regard life as a zero-sum game, where your gain is my loss. I therefore become incapable of generosity and instead breed jealousy and envy.

I am on the defensive. Everything the other person says is assumed to be intended to attack me.

I don't listen. I am thinking of what I am going to say next.

I am not learning. My focus is on things already in my head; things I already know and already believe. This is unfailingly limiting.

I shut myself off to empathy and compassion because I'm too busy plotting my own strategy.

This is what happens when I am intent on understanding the other person:

I am respectful.

I make an effort to assume the other person does not mean to be hostile, if only to contribute to the quality of my own life.

I try to listen to the other person's perspective, because I know I am capable of understanding concepts I don't agree to, if only for mental calisthenics.

I welcome my own growth. Assuming I could be wrong makes me more open to looking at things in a different light, which without exception is to my benefit.

There is no such thing as winning an argument. One player feels like an aggressor. The other diminished and misunderstood. The relationship is eroded, the argument is destined — guaranteed — to be repeated.

If the person I am trying to win an argument against is important to me, then you can see how using the word "winning" is really shortsighted.

If the person I am trying to win an argument against is a stranger, the concept of "winning" puts everyone in the very frame of mind that will least favor me: threatened, closed off, unreceptive.

I don't want to win. I want to understand.

What To Say When You Don't Know What To Say

"I am sorry for your loss" or any other version of it is really important.

I recently had a death in the family and felt that every loving word helped hold me afloat. So show up. It matters.

The best way to say *"I'm sorry for your loss"* is to keep it simple, honest, and if possible, personal. Such as *"I am so sorry for your loss. I will always remember your father's grace and his gift for language".*

Or, if the person didn't know my father *"I am so sorry for your loss and am happy to swing by and give you a hug at your convenience".*

If you want to offer to help, be specific. *"I would love to come drop off some food"* or *"I will be running errands tomorrow - can I pick up something for you?"*

A person grieving is a person overwhelmed by the smallest things so take something off their plate.

Finally, if your gesture does not receive a response make it not matter. It's hard to reply to everyone, even though you feel infinitely grateful for every little thing.

Lust For Learning

I don't understand math.

I blame myself. I suspect I decided it wasn't for me before giving it a fair shake.

This was a mistake.

Mathematicians have access to a world of perfect harmony that I cannot see.

This holds true for every possible subject. There are things to marvel at within languages, outer space, art, biology, insects (their iridescence!), chemistry, cartoons, architecture, the ocean, color, physics, atoms, design and anything else you can conjure.

The more you know, the more beauty is available to you.

The more beauty is available to you, the happier you can be.

Develop a lust for learning. Don't miss a thing.

It's all there, waiting for you.

A Definition Of Forgiveness

To me, forgiveness is wishing the person you are forgiving no ill will.

It does not mean the person occupies the same place in your life; nor does it imply that you carry on as if the transgression never happened.

You can, for example, forgive someone and resolve never to see them again. You don't distance yourself out of anger or spite but out of respect for yourself; out of a healthy need to set new boundaries.

Forgiving someone is not a gift to the person who hurt you but rather a gift to yourself.

The goal of forgiveness is freedom from resentment, bitterness, anger or hatred. Harboring these feelings cannot hurt another person but can cause you great harm. Better to let them go.

Ghosting

I understand "ghosting" to be someone completely disappearing from a relationship without explanation.

If you go out with someone once or twice and then cannot reach the person you were going out with, that to me is not ghosting. There has to be something to walk away from.

In my opinion, ghosting is a terrible form of aggression. You are saying that the other person you once found worthy of your time doesn't even deserve an explanation.

A very close friend of mine was ghosted and was really perplexed and hurt by it. For a few weeks he expected her to suddenly reappear; after which he wondered for months what happened. The end of that relationship was more painful than it needed to be.

How you end a relationship is a part of how you treat others. Everyone deserves clear, honest communication, even if it's painful or uncomfortable.

I don't think this is very healthy for the person doing the ghosting either. Having painful, uncomfortable conversations is an important skill to develop, as is facing difficult things instead of walking away from them.

Dealing with something by turning your back on it is not a good habit to get into.

Think Of Others

I find that life is less frustrating and painful when I stop focusing on myself and start focusing on others.

For me — for me — frustration, anxiety and sadness have a high level of self indulgence.

Every time I feel a bit better I realize that I have shifted my attention to something other than my own struggles.

You Don't Know (What You Want)

If you make lists of what you want, you miss what's right in front of you.

You narrow your choices.

This applies to men and friends and opportunities and walking into a restaurant and ordering before even looking at the menu.

Mick Jagger, who devoured life whole, concluded that *"you can't always get what you want, but you get what you need."*

Open your mind. Open your heart. Give serendipity a chance.

Forget about what you want. Chances are you aren't clear on what that is anyway.

It's Not Yours

I know for sure without an ounce of tragedy that life is loss. That even the most rooted, solid structures are transitory. That everything will change. That trying to hold on will cause suffering. That letting things go will hurt like hell but that pain will move through you instead of lodging inside you.

The single thing I wish for myself, and for you, is that you regard the poetry present all around you with open palms. It's not yours to keep. Nothing is. And therein lies its beauty.

A More Examined Life

We should make it a habit to regularly stop what we are doing, assess our lives and ask ourselves the questions that matter.

Here are some examples:

What am I doing with my life?

Am I happy doing what I am doing? I don't mean happy in a shallow, saccharine way. I mean it in the full sense of the word: purpose, fulfillment, contributing in my own way to leaving the world better than how I found it.

What is it that makes me happy? Very different from the question above. I am very happy preparing delicious food for my boyfriend so it's ready when he gets home. I want to nurture my relationships in every way possible. But writing makes me happy. "Nurturing my relationships" belongs in the previous bullet. "Writing" belongs in this one. The previous one is about evaluating everything we do; the second is about identifying what drives us.

Is my way of perceiving the world hurting me or helping me? There are so many things we cannot change or control. But over time we can have a hand in how we perceive things and how they affect us.

Would I welcome becoming like the people I spend the most time with? Because that's what happens when you spend a lot of time with someone. Who they are rubs off on you.

We could all use a list of good questions that encourage us to live, as Thoreau so eloquently put it, *"a more examined life".*

Evolution

Love evolves.

The love you feel when you initially meet someone is not the same type of love you feel when you have been with them several decades.

It goes from thrilling, to a deep, loving friendship to a companionship.

I think the hardest thing is witnessing this evolution and accepting each phase for what it is instead of wanting to hold on to what it was.

No Escape

We believe we can escape fear by avoiding the circumstances that cause it.

If we are afraid of flying we can resolve not to travel by plane.

If we are afraid of being hurt we can close off our heart.

The truth is the more we adapt our behavior to fear, the more we give it power, and the more it grows.

We cannot let fear make our decisions, because that means it will take over our life.

I read the news today (November 14, 2015) and my heart goes out to the people of Paris, victims of an attack they did not see coming.

And all I can think is I have to get on a plane and go to Paris as soon as I can.

No one can put fear in my heart.

Even if they do, I can refuse to listen.

Balance Is Overrated

We tend to think things will improve…

When we do that.

When we get past that.

When we find that.

But life is now.

Consider this: Roosevelt encourages us *"to know the great enthusiasms, the great devotions"* to *"spend ourselves in a worthy cause".*

Anais Nin noted that *"great art was born of great terrors, great loneliness, great inhibitions".*

"Do not go gentle into that good night" warns Dylan Thomas in this poem that gives me chills every time. *"Rage, rage against the dying of the light".*

My favorite parts of life: falling in love so hard, being irrationally optimistic, feeling completely captivated, inspiration — are completely unbalancing.

Balance is overrated.

If Someone Rejects You

Have you ever read the letter John Steinbeck (the author of <u>Grapes of Wrath</u>, <u>Of Mice and Men</u>, <u>East of Eden</u>) wrote to Thom, his eldest son, after Thom told his dad he was in love?

It's a beautiful letter, clean and simple and true.

My favorite part is the last paragraph:

"And don't worry about losing. If it is right, it happens — the main thing is not to hurry. Nothing good gets away."

I often think about that line: *"Nothing good gets away".*

The best thing to say after someone rejects you is *"Thank you".*

Time is too valuable to waste.

Sunday Blues Are A Sign

The weekend tends to be "what I want to do". The week, punctuated by Monday, tends to be "what I have to do".

One of my life's goals is to do what I need to in order to look forward to Monday morning: quit, find the right job, stop doing things that make me feel dread, or resentful, or depleted.

Life is too short to scorn a seventh of it.

Things You Are Better Off Without

Gossip. Every ounce of energy you spend talking about someone else is energy you are not spending on your own growth.

Besides, anything you ever say about others reveals more about you.

Envy. The sense that others are better off is a fallacy. We are each on our own path and we each have our own challenges, even if they are not always evident.

Jealousy. The illusion that another person can take something away from you inspires a course of action pretty much guaranteed to get you the opposite of whatever it is you are trying to accomplish.

Rivalry. Better to focus on your own path and your own goals and work in harmony with others than to concoct or play into a rivalry that usually succeeds only in throwing you off focus.

Controlling others. The only person you can change, fix, adjust, help or save is yourself.

Hell Is Other People

Imagine a beautiful building.

As you walk through its doors you see a reception desk.

The receptionist is not there, but by the desk is a box of chocolate.

You look around, reach out and take one.

A person you hadn't noticed right behind you says *"Wow! I've always wanted to try that chocolate! How is it?"* and grabs one too.

Now you have an accomplice. You chat about how good the chocolate is.

Mmmm. What a good day this is turning out to be.

But, wait.

What if the person you hadn't noticed behind you instead says *"How could you? How could you take something that doesn't belong to you? I can't believe you just grabbed that!"*

Now you feel uncomfortable.

The receptionist returns to the desk. She glares at you. *"That was not yours."*

You stand there feeling awful.

When Sartre said *"hell is other people"* he noted that we cannot really know ourselves without taking into consideration how we are regarded by others.

If we are judged by another, it becomes a part of our own opinion of ourselves.

Others are so important to us, we cannot complete the puzzle of who we are without them.

This is why he concludes *"hell is other people".*

Sad

I don't understand why we're so afraid of feelings. Happy is acceptable, but sad has to be "addressed". It must "move on". It calls for a solution. But sad is not a problem.

I'm sad and that's OK. I consider sad to be essential. It respects the truth within me, and as such, it is beautiful.

Don't Buy It

I want to raise my hand and say I don't have anything figured out.

Sometimes — OK, often — I don't know what I'm doing. I feel anxious or sad or lost. I fight with Boyfriend, for example, and can't even articulate why we were fighting and I wonder how on Earth I got to be so very bad at relationships. On most nights I have trouble sleeping and sometimes, on bad days, I get up in the morning with a hole in the pit of my stomach and a sense that nothing is in its place or will be again.

I don't write about these things on social media because I want to highlight the good in my life. It's the internet equivalent of smiling for the camera: you're not being hypocritical; you want the photo to represent the moment in a way you'd want to remember it.

More and more people I talk to blurt out some version of *"everyone on Facebook is happier than me"*. It's not just Facebook envy but a form of despair. It's not a fleeting stab of *"I want that"* but rather the deeper, more poisonous *"I fear my life is not good enough"*.

I'm really bothered by the notion that my posts (optimistic, because that is what I am) might be in their minuscule, unintended way contributing to a phenomenon no one would want any part of: the sowing of a collective sense of desperation

(Because you reap what you sow, you know).

A social network at its best is intended to connect us, to open our eyes to another perspective, maybe, hopefully, to inspire and lift us. Not to make us feel (oh, the irony) lost in a delusion of our own fabrication.

I am proud of my life. I have moments where I am really happy. I also cower in fear and make terrible mistakes and fail (the unglamorous kind of fail, not the Michael Jordan kind of fail) and do things I regret. I feel irreparably heartbroken sometimes and then hate myself for being so fragile. The fact that I don't show it doesn't mean it doesn't exist. It's all there, right behind the sunny evidence my friends regularly scroll through.

Go ahead and ask anyone about illness and loss and sorrow and misery. I guarantee no one escapes it. (But who would want to be constantly exposed to that?)

I suppose I could try to start a movement. One that invites us all to regularly be uncensored, more raw. But you can't change the world's behavior. You can only change yourself.

So please, don't buy it. There is no such thing as a charmed life. Perfection is bullshit (not to mention, grossly overrated. The joy is in the flaw).

Don't waste a single second comparing yourself to anything. Do the best you can with the messy, absurd, possibly pointless life you were given and be proud of what you do with it and know that anything dark you go through everyone goes through.

I know I do.

A Particular Brand Of Insecurity

You can love someone and cheat on them. Cheating has nothing to do with your feelings for the other person.

It has nothing to do with anything the other person does or fails to do.

The person that is being cheated on did not somehow fall short of expectations.

I'm going to repeat that because it's important:

It has nothing to do with anything the other person does or fails to do.

The person that is being cheated on did not somehow fall short of expectations.

In my opinion, cheating is the cheater's own internal fracture.

It's an attempt to quench a particular brand of insecurity: the cheater harbors a form of self-doubt temporarily assuaged by cheating.

Then they have to go out and do it again to get the required validation (Hence *"once a cheater, always a cheater"*).

Cheaters are looking for an outside fix for something that can only be addressed from within and they will continue to cheat until they address their internal shortcomings.

Vulnerable

My brother is both tall and wide. He's not overweight; just big. He crouches to get through door frames.

I'm quite small and slender. I feel dwarfed standing next to him.

He once overheard me saying it was not safe to take a bus in Mexico City. He said it was. It took us about 10 minutes to realize that what could feel safe to him did not feel safe to me.

I know not all guys are the same nor do they handle themselves in remotely similar ways.

But I do think it would be helpful for men to understand that a woman's sense of vulnerability is different from theirs and that it is a part of our composition.

I am not saying we are in any way weak. What I am saying is that we are susceptible to feeling threatened.

Baggage

My parents split up when I was five.

They had joint custody of my brother and me. We spent weekdays with my mom, weekends with my dad.

Both wanted to spend more time with us. Both felt sad when the time came to drop us off or pick us up.

My mom cried every week when we said goodbye. My dad was frequently angry when he dropped us off.

Seeing them unhappy made me anxious.

Time went by. I grew up. I moved out. I got married, made my own mistakes.

At 42, I was living alone in an apartment in San Francisco. I met and began dating the man currently known as Boyfriend.

In the first few months of our relationship we were both busy with work. From Monday to Thursday we barely saw each other; typically he'd stay at my place all weekend.

When the time came for him to leave on Sunday night, I felt anxious and weepy. This surprised me. I liked his company, but I too needed to get back to work and loved having the apartment to myself. What was going on?

One night, while we were arguing, Boyfriend says to me

"Dushka, do you realize we invariably fight on Sunday nights?"

I'd like to claim that I put two and two together, but I didn't.

A few months later we were chatting with a therapist who knew nothing about my upbringing. His question was more direct.

"Dushka, can you think of another time in your life when you perhaps had no power and your schedule dramatically shifted on Sunday evenings?"

I was stunned.

This is how I was introduced to the very useful concept of "emotional baggage".

We all carry it.

I have learned that the pattern goes like this:

I realize my feelings are out of proportion to what is actually happening.

I try to figure out what trigger Boyfriend is inadvertently pulling.

I create awareness around this: my baggage — his ability to locate the trigger — what exactly it is that he is bringing up.

I separate my issue from him. They are unrelated.

My feelings dissipate.

Sometimes this takes a few days, sometimes weeks.

After a few months I cannot believe it was something we used to fight about.

For context, I grew up in a family that didn't believe in therapy. Instead, therapy was classified as useless since we were smart enough to work things out for ourselves.

To this I say that if I find something that works for me, I don't need to believe in it to use it.

On a final note, the therapist Boyfriend and I occasionally visit believes that humans unconsciously fall in love with those who push our buttons (or "triggers").

The theory is that if once you were powerless and now you have power and love, you can heal.

I do believe that aside from everything else love is, love is healing.

It has healed me, and it will heal you.

Weakness Or Strength?

What if I told you that every pair of concepts that you regard as opposition are actually one and the same?

Here is an example:

I am intense and committed. Friends tell me I'm the most reliable person they know.

This very same characteristic can also make me overprotective, apprehensive and nosy.

Is this a strength or a weakness? It depends. It depends on what I am applying it to, it depends on the eye (and the mood) of the beholder, and most of all it depends on how it's making me feel (depleted or motivated?).

I accept this gift of intensity as part of who I am but wield it with caution. I know it can make someone feel they are on solid ground or like they are being smothered (sometimes simultaneously).

Our strengths are our weaknesses. If we remove our weaknesses, we do away with not only what makes us who we are but precisely what we need to make us successful.

Deal Breaker

I come from a conservative country and have a conservative upbringing.

In the very beginning of our relationship my boyfriend told me he was going to take a trip with a friend.

A *girl* friend.

And that they were staying in the same room.

I FLIPPED OUT.

I told him *"If you travel with a woman friend and stay in the same room with her, I'm out".*

To which he responded *"If you threaten me, I'm out".*

I grabbed the handle of the door of my apartment and opened the door really wide.

He walked out.

We later worked out that what people say is not always what they mean.

He was saying: *I am going to travel with a woman friend and you can't stop me.*

He meant: *Please don't try to control me or my behavior.*

I was saying: *If you travel with a woman friend and stay in the same room with her I am out.*

I meant: *Please don't hurt me.*

You cannot control another person.

Relationships are so hard. You have to accept your feelings and decide what you can live with.

My boyfriend doesn't stay in the same room with his female friends when he travels because he knows it would make me uncomfortable.

But he knows that he can.

While this is still difficult for me, I feel better about it now.

I know him and trust him so to me it's no longer a deal breaker.

Your Inner Dialogue

Compassion is the ability to step out of your own skin and experience a situation from another's point of view.

It's setting your own interests aside and replacing them with somebody else's.

Inside my head, when I talk to myself, I tend to furiously represent my own interests.

You told me you'd be here at 7:00 and I've been waiting for you for over an hour.

In my head the argument heats up. It escalates.

It's inconsiderate. It shows no respect for my time.

If I change the dialogue inside my head, if I get out of my own way, I can see the picture a lot more clearly.

He is not late on purpose. Why would he do that? He is usually punctual. He must be so stressed.

If you allow your inner dialogue to represent the person you tend to argue with, life becomes more harmonious, more peaceful, easier to understand.

Soul Mate

Anais Nin said *"we have been poisoned by fairy tales."*

"Soul mate" is a romantic notion that contributes to us developing unrealistic expectations.

There are many many wonderful people out there who would make a great significant other, after which you really have to work on yourself and your own baggage to make the relationship something worthy of a romance novel.

Soul mates are not found. They are created.

The Right Dosage

I'm an introvert and I love people.

For me it's just a matter of the right dosage.

Here are some things that allow me to enjoy being with people more:

A finite time frame. I like knowing I can leave quickly if I've had enough. So, *"let's have tea"* works better for me than a dinner with a 7 course tasting menu.

Small numbers of people. One other person, maybe two. Or two couples. This tires me out less than having to, say, "work a room".

Social media. The ability to network, write, exchange ideas, learn about others — without ever having to interact with anyone in person. Yesssss.

Discover the awesomeness of extroverts. Yes. They can exhaust me. But they are also animated and talkative and charming and carry the conversation so I don't have to. One of my best friends is an extreme extrovert. I take him everywhere. He's better than any fashion accessory.

Resting when you need to. I stroll out into the balcony, step out into the hall, hide in the restroom. Sometimes I need to be alone for weeks, but often 10 minutes will do wonders.

Make sure you always have an escape plan. I get very tired (and stressed) when I can't see a place to retreat. I never invite people to my apartment, for example (will they ever leave?), and I never travel with lots of friends (Friends: *Let's all rent a cabin together and go skiing!* Me: *Noooooo.*).

Avoid noisy, rowdy places. Bars and parties don't work for me but if the place is quiet I can stay much longer.

Finally, know that there is peace within you. Both in your introversion and in embracing the fact that you're perfect the way you are.

The best thing you can do for yourself: never waste time wishing you were different.

Serendipity

Serendipity.

First of all, look at it. It's such a beautiful word.

The etymology does not come from Latin or Greek. Through a Google search I learned that a man named Horace Walpole derived it from The Three Princes of Serendip, a fairy tale in which the heroes *"were always making discoveries, by accident or sagacity, of things they were not in quest of."*

According to the Webster Dictionary, serendipity is defined as the phenomenon through which you find something wonderful that you were not looking for; discovering something amazing by chance.

While luck is more democratic, serendipity seems to be reserved for a particular kind of person: perhaps one who is receptive to something unexpected.

You have to start out by being open to the notion that anything is possible.

I believe there are a few things we do that affect serendipity — things that reduce our chances of happening upon something delightful.

Overbooking or overplanning. If you leave nothing to chance, you shut out serendipity.

Being constantly in a rush. Serendipity needs time to play.

Constantly looking at your phone. Our destiny often shows up in the form of serendipity. A chance encounter in the street. A glance in a café.

I wonder how many things we are passing by that are supposed to be happening; what we are doing to the fabric of our fate by never looking up from our mobile devices.

The Dream Paradox

You know you are pursuing the right dream because it makes you feel happy right now. You forget to plan for the future and feel like the present moment is all you need.

Then you can trust that whatever happens next will take care of itself.

Looks Like Fun

The times when I have felt I am missing out have been the times when I have not been happy with myself or what I'm doing.

Here are some things that look really fun but that I would not be missing out on because I don't find them fun:

A large group of people traveling together (as an introvert traveling with others is very stressful and exhausting).

A bar: Rowdy, noisy, crowded. I'd much much rather be home in the company of a good book.

A party: I crouch in a corner and wonder how soon I can leave.

There are things I do that are really, really fun. I don't want to miss out on them but if someone really extroverted saw my photos they would probably be OK not being a part of them:

Drinking coffee and reading the news.

Writing.

Reading.

Cooking (OK. Watching my boyfriend cook while I loiter around the kitchen tasting things that aren't ready).

When I am true to myself and what interests me, the feeling that someone else is having more fun than me goes away completely.

The Ideal Relationship

Imagine for a second that a relationship — any relationship — is a very large, fragile, unwieldy, lopsided, priceless object.

And that calling it "ideal" is equivalent to perching it precariously on a high, thin, narrow, rickety pedestal.

Relationships are much more secure if you place them down here on the floor.

Right on this dusty, messy arena we call life.

How To Destroy A Relationship

John Gottman, A marriage and relationship expert, says there are 4 things that are practically guaranteed to destroy any relationship.

The first one is contempt. This can be disdain, eye rolls, walking away, sighing with exasperation. It makes your significant other feel you are disgusted with him. *Ugh. I cannot believe you did that. How could you?*

The second is criticism: *You never do this right. Why did you not think that through?* This is when you attack the person rather than what they are doing.

The third is defensiveness: You begin by assuming the other person is attacking you (instead of trying to explain things to you) and defend everything — *No I didn't! I would not do that! That is not what I intended!* — blocking rather than listening. This eliminates a spirit of collaboration.

The fourth is my personal kryptonite and it's called stonewalling. This is when you are trying to talk to someone you love, when you are hurt and upset and needing desperately to be understood (*You don't have to agree with me. Just understand me!*), and the other person shuts down, does not talk, turns away or leaves.

A relationship takes two and you are left alone.

Being stonewalled is, to me, a domestic form of hell. Engage with me. Look at me. Talk to me. Fight with me.

Care enough to fight with me.

Don't just leave me here.

Gottman goes on to add that most problems between a couple stay forever. You have slightly different versions of the same argument over and over. The arguments are not what harm you (even if he never takes out the garbage): it's the way you handle them.

Learning to accept yourself and the other person, while staying close — connected — is what makes you strong. It's what makes the relationship survive.

Google "Gottman, The Four Horsemen of the Apocalypse" if you want to read this in his words. The above is my interpretation.

Fight well. Fight fairly. It's not fun, but it's necessary.

Tips For Dating An Introvert

I'm an introvert.

On a first date I need two things:

Quiet

The ability to connect with the person I am on a date with.

To be clear, I need something to connect over, rather than something to connect away from.

This would rule out libraries and bookstores, and would eliminate movies (We can visit a bookstore or go watch a movie when we know each other better).

Some ideas for our date:

Food. I can show you a list of the most awesome things to taste in San Francisco and you can pick one (or three).

Tea. We can go to the lobby of a fancy hotel and order high tea (We can legitimately use the word "crumpet").

A game. Are you good at playing ping pong, paddle tennis, pool or at bowling? I'm not, and I'd love to learn. Show me.

A museum. Maybe a children's museum so we can touch everything (I like textures).

The botanical garden. A stroll through stunning greenery, crazy looking exotic plants and yummy smelling herbs. The San Francisco Botanical Garden is a beauty. Sometimes they hide pianos in nooks so anyone can play.

Window shopping. I'm not a big shopper but I love looking. Over the holiday season I like going to street and art fairs just to see what people are making.

Coffee. Because, coffee.

We can listen to music. Not at a concert (I don't like either crowds or noise). But, how about two pairs of headphones plugged into the same device? *Grab your things. I've come to take you home.* (Bring a blanket).

Itchy Sweater

Have you ever watched The Big Bang Theory?

Sheldon feels extremely uncomfortable with certain things that others don't even register (lack of order, pending items, rented movies that haven't been returned, arguments that make no sense to him, etc.).

If you don't notice something or it doesn't bother you it's hard to empathize because you are blind to it.

In one episode Sheldon suggests Leonard wear a very itchy sweater to truly understand how uncomfortable he feels.

We would all be better human beings if we kept itchy sweaters in our closet for such occasions.

As an introvert, when a friend insists that I attend her party *"because I'll have so much fun"* she could wear an itchy sweater the whole time we are there.

Not at all as retaliation. Just because it's awesome to be understood.

Inner Dragon

In the context of daily struggles, this right here is one of my biggest.

I tend towards wanting to be alone. In a way this suits me but in another I love my friends and want to spend time with them.

Tragically, I am enriched by the company of others.

This is what works for me (sometimes):

I look at my entire week and try to balance it. My job is very social so I tend to not go out from Monday to Friday; then limit myself to one social engagement per weekend (or every other weekend, as the case may be). I've learned that feeling "peopled out" is cumulative.

I keep social engagements to a format I can handle: Tea, dinner with one other person, or getting together with a small group.

I seldom have dinners at my house. I need to know I can easily retreat (Although I have been known to end a get-together at my house by getting up and saying "it's time for you all to leave now").

I avoid parties but when I have to go I find a corner to sit in and talk to whoever is closest instead of "working the room". I'd rather have one or two good conversations than flit around trying to engage in small talk, which burns me out within 1.2

146

minutes (on a really good day).

My boyfriend and I have developed a complex, secret code that I will hereby reveal: *"Do you think it's time to go, babe?"* Actually means *"get me out now"*, and cannot ever be countered with *"10 more minutes."*

My boyfriend understands me. We were at a party recently and I was in the middle of a conversation, quite engaged. He came up to the corner I was sitting in and said *"I'm looking at you and think we need to go"*. Half a minute later my *"I'm social"* switch flipped to *"Now. I need to leave now."* He somehow detects this early and plots an exit route before I realize what's happening (I bet you it's that my hair gets really frizzy).

Despite my best efforts, I do feel like striking this "balance" is near impossible. Like you, I am complicated and moody, don't know exactly what I need, and have discovered my "limit" is a moving target (Or, wait. Maybe this is just me).

If I am caught in a social setting "peopled out" I can be short, rude or harsh. I feel terrible afterwards.

This "need for space" is one of my inner dragons, but venturing out into the open air is good for her unkempt, fire spitting soul.

Do It Here

Running away is, for me, a recurring fantasy.

"You can't run away forever" sings Meatloaf, *"but there is nothing wrong with getting a good head start".*

I used to live within walking distance of the Pacific Ocean in Montara, California.

I longed to get away and called up one of my best friends, who lives in Costa Rica.

"Yes" she said *"Please! Come stay as long as you want!"*

She then added the words she knew I'd find impossible to resist. *"I'll feed you!"*

I packed a toothbrush, a notebook, a bathing suit, flip flops, a pair of jeans and a few t-shirts.

I jumped on a plane and flew six hours away from my life.

I landed in San José and drove on a highway and then across mostly dirt roads to the place I was staying in.

The journey took a full day. Upon arrival, I opened the car door, got out, stretched, and walked up to the edge of the balcony to take in the view.

There it was. The exact same ocean.

There are some very valid reasons to run away. But most of them (for me) have to do with something inside me.

This implies that no matter how much I run, no matter how far I go, I take it with me.

What I'm running away from will be anywhere I go.

Better to just take care of it here.

Better to just address it now.

Should I Change For You?

When someone asks something of me (boss, significant other, parent) I ask myself the following:

Would this be good for me? Help me grow? Be a better person? Would this effort improve my life across other areas?

Or

Is this request akin to me becoming someone I am not?

If the request falls in the first category, I work on it. It might be uncomfortable, but this is how we grow. This is how we look back and marvel at how far we've come.

If the request falls into the second category, my answer is no.

My Grief

Grief is personal. Each person grieves differently and the stages happen in no particular order or not at all or all at once. When my dad died helpful people asked me why on Earth I wasn't crying.

I didn't cry at all, not a single tear, for the first couple of weeks. After that I did, but never as much as would be considered by the general population the "correct amount".

Rather than sitting in a corner to sob what I wanted was to run. It was a fight, or a flight. It didn't feel like I had lost someone. It felt like I was in danger.

The whole world is on another planet far, far away from yours. You learn to respect the cadence of your planet.

It felt like time had slowed way down for me. I would compare it to being suspended underwater, complete with muffled sounds, languid movement and refracted light. But the rest of the world keeps moving, fast, and the sheer frenzy of it exerts an unintended, relentless, exhausting pressure.

My dad died December 15, 2014, and through a few weeks that mostly felt unreal, everywhere I went cheery people would ask *"How is your holiday going?" "What are you doing for New Years?" "Are you enjoying your time off?"* and every time it caught me completely unprepared. It wiped me out.

Simple things can be hard. It forced me to be patient with myself. We had to go through and sort my father's things: his house, his clothes, his drawers and files. It might have been easier had we not felt like plunderers, invaders transgressing on a privacy he always guarded with such sacredness.

People tell you *"things get better"* (and so many other ridiculous things). I learned to set boundaries. You'd think "things will get better" would bring someone solace. But here is the catch: in a way, your feelings are part of what is left of the other person. As such, you don't want to get better. Not right away, anyway. Also, it feels like feeling better too quickly would be an act of betrayal. So saying "things will get better" can be an affront.

People say *"don't be sad"*. I learned to give my feelings the space they needed. I don't understand why we are so afraid of feelings. Happy is OK, but sad has to be "addressed". It must "move on". It calls for a "solution". But sad is not a problem.

I'm sad, and I'm not ready to not be sad. I am going to sit here with my big bag of sad for as long as it wants to hang out with me. I consider sad to be essential. It respects the truth within me, and as such, it is beautiful.

(Of course I am not talking about clinical depression or a grief that has stayed with a person for whatever length is no longer "normal". I am talking about natural feelings associated with losing someone you deeply loved and wanting to sort through every one in your own way. For clinical depression, talk to a doctor. I'm no doctor.)

People say *"cheer up"*. Or even *"suck it up"*.

I know they mean well, but this feels like you are being slapped. It's a form of aggression. This sadness is mine, and you can't touch it. So back off. But thank you.

You feel (and this is so horrible it makes me cry just to write it) like you are going to forget the person that you lost. You learn that feelings don't need to make sense.

152

It's so shocking for a person to be there and then to not be there that it feels like everything they were will disappear. I fear I won't remember my father's voice or the glint in his eye or his clean smell or his soft white handkerchiefs or the way he put his foot up on something to tie his shoelace or the frequently astounding things he used to say when I asked for his opinion.

So what does a grieving person want? For the whole world to grind to a halt? Why, yes. We want, in words of W.H. Auden, to *"stop all the clocks".* We want *"an airplane to scribble on the sky the message He is Dead".* We want *"the stars put out, the moon packed up, the sun dismantled, the ocean poured away."*

But we understand this isn't reasonable (to you), so ask instead for patience as we very slowly step back out into this new world that no longer includes a person who once determined its shape.

Goodbye Fashion

I have come across many articles that explore the notion of wearing the same thing every day.

Can I say goodbye to fashion trends and never look back?

I found what worked for me and wear (slightly different versions of) the same outfit every day.

When I find something on sale that is easy to wear (soft, matchable, comfortable, flattering) I get more than one.

I wear a basic dress with different boots, a different wrap, a different sweater or a different coat and nobody ever notices (except sometimes to say *"nice boots"!*)

I rarely buy clothes. I seldom go shopping. My closet is simple and I wear everything in it.

For trips, I never need more than a carry on suitcase.

Aside from the amount of money I save on clothes, it saves me time and stress every morning (not to mention the time, effort and stress inherent in shopping trips).

There are so many other decisions I'd rather be focusing my energy on rather than *OH MY GOD WHAT AM I GOING TO WEAR TO MY MEETING.*

How Can I Save Him?

"Trying to save someone (from their weaknesses)" is a form of self-centeredness disguised as generosity. It implies you can do something for someone that they can't do for themselves and that you somehow know what that is.

The concept that we need saving is a fallacy. The real name for it is codependency, which is never healthy and is destined to end badly.

Implicit in "trying to save someone" is that you don't accept who that person already is. It means you want to influence or change them, because somehow you know better.

The tendency to try to save another will also ensure you attract the wrong person: the kind not ready for a relationship.

I want to be happy with someone who is already happy and wants to share that happiness, rather than assume the responsibility of someone who is expecting to be made happy by me (I'm confused enough trying to make myself happy. I'm all I can handle.).

Putting yourself in the position of a "savior" or a hero makes you feel like you are doing something good, but believe me when I tell you it's poison for both you and the person allegedly being saved.

The moment you stop trying to influence, change or rescue

others you will amazed at how much time, life, energy and love you have left over to do your primary task: fix yourself. Improve yourself. Save yourself.

Technique

Boyfriend and I had just started living together and I really wanted to be the best possible girlfriend.

I was thinking about the inevitable discrepancy between what is most important to me and where I put my time.

From Monday to Friday, I spend roughly 3 hours a day with my significant other and 10 hours a day at work.

I resolved to make sure I had energy for him at the end of the day: to welcome him home with a hug and a smile; to talk about our day over a nice dinner sitting at the dining room table rather than in tired fragments mumbled during commercial breaks.

So I hear his keys rattle against the keyhole. I open the door wide and hug him and kiss him and welcome him home.

"Honey" he says *"could you let me put my stuff down and take my jacket off and give me a few minutes to catch my breath?"*

I immediately feel like he's not happy to see me.

I was telling a friend about this calamitous turn of events and he asks: *"Dushka, why are you taking this so personally?"*

Me: *Huh?*

Him: *Is it possible that Boyfriend has things going on before his arrival to your house? That he had a long day, work to get through, traffic to sit through? You are a total introvert. Surely you understand when someone else needs space?*

Me: *Oh.*

Technique #1 to develop emotional strength:

Realize that nothing is personal.

This "separation" between how another person reacts and you will improve your relationships, make you less self-centered, reduce unnecessary drama and forever set you free.

Cocktail

I feel truly happy every day.

It has helped me a lot to understand that feelings come mixed with other feelings, rather than the expectation that feelings arise distilled and pure.

A single feeling is rarely felt in isolation.

True happiness can coexist with other things and be just as true.

Your Comfort Zone

Have you ever been on a roller coaster ride?

Do you remember what you felt as the car you were on inched its way to the very top? That split second of suspension before the hair raising descent, a feeling of elated vertigo?

You're scared — shaky, heart pounding, panting — but excited too; roiling anticipation.

Putting yourself outside your comfort zone feels like varying degrees of that.

It means going for things you have always wanted but didn't because you were afraid.

These are not necessarily things that risk your physical safety but rather what might make you more vulnerable to failure.

You realize that you can't grow unless you give up being complacent.

Ask any bodybuilder what happens when you do the exact same workout every day: your body, efficient, intelligent, gets used to it. Your progress stops.

As much as we crave comfort and routine, we were designed to be kept challenged, not to be kept comfortable.

Obviously, what makes each person uncomfortable varies

greatly depending on the individual.

Some examples:

Asking him/her out.

Raising your hand in class: you always know the answer but are nervous to speak up and it's time that you did.

Living alone because you know you can even though you feel you can't so I guess you just have to show yourself.

Traveling alone.

Asking for a raise not just for the money but as a first step to finding your voice.

Moving from a safe job to a job that stretches you when everyone tells you it's crazy but you know in your heart it would be crazier not to.

Deciding to leave. Or resolving to stay.

Disappointing someone who loves you to be true to yourself.

Finally saying *"I love you".* Finally saying *"no".* Finally saying *"yes".*

Trusting yourself. Trusting again. Because if you don't trust, you assure me, your heart is safe; but tell me, what good is a safe heart?

Don't waste a perfectly good heart by keeping it safe.

Trying out zip-lining when you've always been afraid of heights; jumping off the platform and zipping head first over the river because you know what they say about vertigo: it's not that you're afraid to fall.

It's that you want to fly.

To Increase Productivity, Do Less

Set time aside to do nothing.

Being too busy is a creativity killer.

Silence will inspire you.

Peace will inspire you.

Quiet will inspire you.

A good way to start might be to set aside 10 minutes a day, three times a day to sit somewhere quiet and breathe.

Or to take a walk during which you don't have to talk, check your phone or run errands.

Your Personal Brand

The use of the term "personal brand" makes me cringe. It's not just that it sounds ego-driven. It's that calling it that means that we're missing something essential.

Wanting a personal brand assumes we need a brand to shape us. Really, it's the other way around. We design, give shape to, determine a brand.

A "brand" was originally intended to anthropomorphize a company by giving it a personality, in order to make it unique, to tell it apart from others. You, a human being, already have a personality. You come equipped with it at birth. You don't want to develop a brand. What you want is to identify the brand (if we must call it that) that you already have.

To do this, you have a single question to answer. What is it that you do that would be of service? To rephrase, what do you have to give to others? Can you articulate that? Think beyond your current job and even your next one. Think more along the lines of what matters to you, what you love, what you'd like to leave behind.

In the words of David Brooks, who wrote the brilliant article "The Moral Bucket List", *"Consider less your résumé virtues, and think about your eulogy virtues".* First because these are what most faithfully make you you — but also because this is what both individuals and the world need the most.

Focusing on what we want to leave behind is also the antidote to our increasing terror of becoming irrelevant.

"Relevance" means "connected," as in "connected to the matter at hand." It comes from the Latin *"to lift, to raise up."* Relevance has to do with real life. Our secret, regular acts of heroism make us relevant. Our relevance is in being human, in loving, in being a part of our family, our community, in showing up. In other words, you don't really need to "struggle to remain" something you already are.

Much like the concept of "a personal brand", "struggling to remain relevant" is a false premise: it misleads you into assuming "relevance" is defined by clicks or likes.

The only way to escape this soul sapping like-chasing pathology is to operate from a place of conviction (I would say "authenticity" but feel we've beaten that one beyond recognition).

Put simply, it means you should spend time doing what makes you happy. It means you should do and say things because they are important to you.

"Do what you love" is not an idealistic platitude. It's tied to competence, productivity, even relevance. When you love doing something, you want to do it a lot. You are — almost accidentally — practicing, improving, exploring, learning, expanding, all the time. There is no way to remain competitive against someone who loves what you slog through.

This practice of, in a sense, moving towards a sense of purpose through doing what matters to you, what makes you fulfilled in this moment, even if you are doing so inch by inch, trial and error, will unequivocally identify you. It will also make companies that you work for better for having you — and this energy you bring — be a part of them.

Who you are and what you do are meant to be cohesive. What you do all those hours that you are in the office amounts, in effect, to your life's work. To quote Annie Dillard, *"how you spend your days is, of course, how you spend your life."*

I don't mean to imply that all of this is easy. It will, in fact, be the hardest, most important thing you do; an ever-evolving series of experiments that will take the rest of your life. But you will be creating something that feeds you, that provides a clear direction towards your own evolution, and that (hopefully) leaves things better than how you found them.

It's about so much more than "managing your brand." It's how we each choose to contribute to make ourselves better, and in turn making the world a better place.

Fear

In his book <u>The Gift of Fear</u>, Gavin De Becker says that humans have been given marvelous, complex, highly evolved instincts designed to keep us out of harm's way.

The problem is that we override internal alarms in the name of being "polite" or "reasonable".

He illustrates his point with the following example: Say that you are waiting for an elevator. The doors open and you see someone already inside that sends a chill down your spine (or turns your stomach into a knot).

But, it would be so rude, even offensive, to stare at the person and then refrain from getting on the elevator, right?

You decide to ignore your own message, telling yourself that being afraid of someone you've never met makes no sense and determine that it instead makes a lot of sense to get into a small, sound proof, inescapable metal box with someone you instinctively are afraid of.

This story blew me away. Because I make these types of decisions all the time: doing things against my better judgment in an attempt to "make sense". Making an elaborate intellectual effort to convince myself my instincts cannot possibly be right. And, I love my instincts. They are so often correct! They were put there to help me.

I've decided they deserve more respect than this. Not just mine — everyone's. So I invite you to listen to yours too.

166

How My Parents Got Me To Love Books

They led by example. Kids like doing what their parents do. If they see you reading, they will want to read next to you.

Integrate reading into everything. Some examples: If someone likes pancakes, look up how to make different versions of them. If you go to the park, look up more information of the dog you saw, or the insect (And by "look up" I mean books, not Google).

Have books back up conversations. An atlas is a great example of this. Where exactly is Fiji, anyway? Or an encyclopedia of animals. What is a platypus? Is the plural platypie?

Read to them before you go to bed. Stop when they are in a really suspenseful part. Promise you will continue the next night.

Go to bookstores. Explore different books together. Make sure they are age appropriate and that the topic interests them.

Ask them to give you a book for your birthday. Then return the favor.

Best Case Scenario

I will immediately, unfailingly go to the worst possible case scenario.

It's not that I'm a pessimist. I'm an optimist who concluded long ago that to accurately assess a situation I needed to ask *"What's the worst that could happen?"* The assumption is that if I have evaluated the worst, I will be ready for anything.

I have discovered that this is flawed reasoning, because:

It's impossible to prepare for *anything*, given that the combinations of unfortunate things that can happen are, I'm sorry to say, infinite. So, when something bad does happen, rather than being "ready" I sit there bleary eyed and wild-haired wondering how on Earth I did not see it coming.

Operating in worst case scenario mode leads me to live in a perpetual state of heightened anxiety (It's no wonder, since I inhabit a nightmarish kind of place).

The lethally ironic blow? The exercise completely dulls my instincts, so that when something happens I cannot read my most trusty tool (my internal compass) because I've dulled it with a flood of possible scenarios that do not take place.

Ultimately, what I end up without is faith. Because I'm so busy looking ahead at likely disasters that I fail to notice all of the times that what I was expecting did not occur.

So I'm now in the middle of the most difficult exercise: training every day to resist taking my well tread, completely cleared away path that leads to worst case scenarios; and instead choosing to open through dense jungle the trail that no one has ever set foot on of trying to conceive the best that could happen.

Saying this doesn't come naturally to me would be an understatement. It scares me, because it feels like I an setting myself up to be ambushed, hurt or disappointed.

But instead of living through the heartbreak of all the catastrophes that have only happened in my (hyperactive) imagination, I hope to live through the joy of a thousand perfect (and equally plausible) outcomes.

This way, when crisis strikes, at least I won't be exhausted.

I Can't Live If Living Is Without Me

Tell me, I was saying. *Tell me who it is you want me to be.*

Just please don't leave me.

We think it's romantic — even required — to change who we are in the name of love.

But if we change to be better suited for the person that we love, how do we not lose track of who we are?

And if we lose track of who we are, what is left of us to love?

Everything we have been taught about love is wrong.

Through fairy tales and music and movies we are bombarded by consistent notions about what love is: *I can't live if living is without you.*

And we say implausible things in the name of love: *I will do anything for you. I need you. I cannot live without you. You are my everything.*

You complete me.

Here is the thing. These concepts are not evidence of true love. They are evidence of desperation and dependency. They sow unhealthy patterns that get worse as we get older, more ingrained, more difficult to break.

We scatter pieces of our identity and independence in the name of the very things love is not.

Love does not leave you empty.

Why is it that we are so willing — eager, desperate — to turn our backs on the undeniable, beautiful fact that we were created whole?

I was created whole.

Heartbreak is so incredibly painful it has made me wish that I was dead.

When you are in the grip of that feeling of devastation and emptiness there is only one person to turn to: yourself.

Love yourself with that same ferocity. Turn this passionate declaration "I am willing to do anything in the world" on yourself.

Be willing to do anything in the world for you.

Listen to lyrics of songs and deliberately change them.

I can't live if living is without me.

Keep doing that until you feel the grace and dignity that is true love.

Until you cannot see any other alternative but walking away from anyone who doesn't love you the way you deserve to be loved.

Until the person that you love does not need you, can easily live without you, is utterly complete already, but wants very much to stay.

Jinx

A jinx is something that is supposed to bring you bad luck.

It has somehow become very ingrained into the way we live our lives.

Here is an example.

My friend, who has been looking for a job for months, calls me.

Her: *"I got a call from my recruiter! She told me the job offer was on its way!"*

Me: *"Congratulations! Let's go celebrate!"*

Her: *"Oh, no no no. I haven't gotten the offer yet so I wouldn't want to jinx it".*

People: There is no such thing as a jinx. Or a spell. Or a hex. Or a curse.

If my friend had accepted my invitation, we would have celebrated her new job twice: once when she initially got the news, then again with the arrival of the offer.

Life is short. It's meant to be abundantly, frequently, perhaps even excessively celebrated.

Resolve to celebrate with abandon.

Throw out this notion of a jinx.

Don't ever postpone or limit joy.

Self-acceptance

Finding happiness is a journey. And because everything changes and you change you have to start this journey over and over again. It's already hard enough.

A good way to start on this complex, wonderful process is to take a good look at what you are and accept it. From this place of loving acceptance you can find people like you who define happiness in the same way.

You stop asking questions like: *Am I normal? Is there something wrong with me? Should I try to be something other than what I am?* (The answers are: yes, no and please no)

The worst way to start on this complex, wonderful process is to force yourself to be something you are not. You will be met with the strongest, most primal, most desperate resistance. You will end up surrounded by the wrong people (for you). You will condemn yourself to perpetual inadequacy. You will wake up one morning wondering how on Earth you ended up in the wrong life.

Improving yourself — striving to be a better person — is essential to happiness.

Changing yourself — trying to be something you aren't will make you angry, bitter, resentful, hopeless, lonely.

Believe me when I tell you who you already are is perfect. Go find that. Accept that. Love that. Amplify it. Be proud of it. Hold it up so others like you can find you.

Unrequited Love

Love feels like we have been plugged into a higher power. We even look radiant.

Being in love is such a delicious, life- affirming gift.

But we suffocate love.

It makes us feel vulnerable. We know we could get terribly hurt; so we expect — demand — that this love be returned. We want to be comfortable and safe. We want to control the situation and control others. We want a guarantee of reciprocation.

But the truth is we are never really safe. We cannot control others.

Alas. There are no guarantees.

If the other person doesn't love you back, it's natural to want to let your heart grow hard, to protect it from getting hurt in the future.

The thing is, you will get hurt no matter what.

The only alternative is to learn that love doesn't have to be returned.

You can rejoice in being in love no matter what the other person feels for you.

You need to, in Pema Chodron's words, *"keep your heart soft".*

"Keep breaking your heart" she says *"until it opens".*

Can you sit with all this love you feel and just hold it, reaping its benefits, taking in its energy, being infused by it, inspired by it, without wanting anything back?

This is a very difficult practice that you work at through compassion, empathy, joy and meditation.

(And some days suck and nothing works and you just want to call so you can hear his voice and hang up and cry.)

About The Author

Dushka Zapata has worked in the communications industry for over 20 years running agencies like Edelman and Ogilvy in Silicon Valley. She specializes in coaching executives to talk to media, give presentations, and refine what they want to say.

She lives in San Francisco with her Boyfriend, who makes her coffee every morning.

Made in the USA
Las Vegas, NV
24 November 2023

81395030R00114